MISS MANNERS'
BASIC TRAINING™:
THE RIGHT
THING TO SAY

MISS MANNERS'
BASIC TRAINING™

THE RIGHT
THING TO SAY

JUDITH MARTIN

CROWN PUBLISHERS, INC.

NEW YORK

Published by Crown Publishers, Inc., 201 East 50th Street, New York, New York 10022. Member of the Crown Publishing Group.

Random House, Inc. New York, Toronto, London, Sydney, Auckland
www.randomhouse.com/

CROWN and colophon are trademarks of Crown Publishers, Inc.

Printed in the United States of America

Design by Debbie Glasserman

Library of Congress Cataloging-in-Publication Data
Martin, Judith, 1938–
Miss Manners' basic training : the right thing to say / by Judith
Martin — 1st ed.
Includes index.
(alk. paper)
1. Conversation.   2. Etiquette.   I. Title.
BJ2121.M356   1998
395.5'9—dc21   97-28967

ISBN 0-609-60051-6

10 9 8 7 6 5

FOR EUNICE AND WILLIE RIDDICK

There is no form strong enough to express Miss Manners' gratitude to David Hendin, Ann Hughey, Ann Patty and R.G.M.

CONTENTS

MISS MANNERS'
BASIC TRAINING™:
THE RIGHT
THING TO SAY

CHAPTER 1

GENERAL PRINCIPLES

THE WRONG THING TO SAY

Originality turned out to be a bad idea.

Not that Miss Manners would mind occasionally seeing a movie that wasn't based on a movie about making a movie, or going to an experimental theater that tried any experiment other than "Let's see if we can shock them by showing them body parts." But in everyday life, originality won't do. We've tried it.

In the heady era of believing that we are all born bursting with creativity, the conventional phrases society uttered for marking the conventional events of life were cast aside as insufficient and insincere. It no longer seemed enough to say "Congratulations" to the happy, "I'm terribly sorry" to the sad, and "Get well soon" to the sick. Something more inspired seemed necessary.

But what? The suggestion—not a noticeably original idea, by the way—was that people should consult their feelings and then improvise remarks based on their emotions. Uninhibited by the unimaginative dictates of etiquette, they would produce fresh heart-to-heart communication—a veritable flow of uniquely personal empathy that would make the world a better place.

Only they didn't and it isn't. Searching their hearts, most people came up with the idea of talking about themselves or of critiquing others.

They took friends' milestones and predicaments as opportunities to recount their own past experiences, thus eclipsing anybody else's current situation by putting the spotlight on themselves. When they did think about what was happening to their friends, they expressed how envious or how relieved they were that it wasn't happening to them.

Or they interpreted announcements and silence alike as license to probe for intimate details and to tell one and all what was wrong with them and how they could live their lives better. Their own failings they saved for strangers, whose mere presence—even strangers on airplanes with books over their faces—they took as invitations to unburden themselves of their most intimate confessions.

They stopped apologizing because they had already forgiven themselves, and they dropped words such as "please," "excuse me" and "thank you," which only served to appease others, not to express their own feelings. It occurred to them that other people's disappointed expectations were those people's problem.

Miss Manners does not for a minute think that all people are selfish—or even that all rude people are. Relieved of etiquette, even the highest sentiments can be offensive.

Those with the strongest moral fervor became, when relieved of the polite pretense of respect for the opinions of others, the most obnoxious. Even those most conscious of not wanting to offend helped lower the tone of society by pretending not to mind vulgarity and insults.

The most emotionally devasting remarks were made to those who most genuinely wanted to enter into other people's joys or sorrows. Under the mistaken notion that the right words could fundamentally alter the situation for the better, they tried to make the newly bereaved cheerful and the newly engaged cautious. Or knowing that such consolation and counsel had cruel results, they admitted they didn't know what to say—and offended people with their silence.

Etiquette can provide people with the right thing to say—but not because it's so adorably creative (although heaven knows it sometimes has to be to get through the situations people throw at it nowadays). It is because it expresses its feelings in the time-tested ways that it knows will be appreciated and understood.

ATTEMPTS TO IMPROVE ON THE CONVENTIONAL

Why would anyone say "Congratulations" to a couple who has just announced an engagement or the expected birth of a child? Congratulating people is what is now done at funerals. Anyone who has suffered a loss can expect to be told:

"It's really a blessing, you know."
"You must be relieved it's over."
"You're lucky it didn't drag out longer."
"Thank God he isn't suffering any more."
"You must realize that it's all for the best."

Those who are most skillful at comforting the bereaved with such congratulatory statements are able to go for a second round, Miss Manners has observed. When they have elicited a fresh outburst of woe, they congratulate the mourners again, this time for "dealing with" or "working through" their grief, or tell them what stage they are at, as if grief were a subway stop. Thus, they have the enormous satisfaction of having done something for their friends. Driven them to tears.

This custom doesn't leave anything to say to happy people. If a death is a blessing, what is a birth? If people are better off when their relatives die, what can they reasonably expect to feel when they acquire new relatives?

Miss Manners is not complaining of a vacuum. Those who disdain the boring old customs of etiquette, which admittedly often require saying the obvious, have developed a variety of new conventions for giving the fortunate the same emotional opportunities as those fortunate enough to be unfortunate. Here are some of the things people routinely say now, to comfort those who have decided to get married:

"It's about time."

"Let me tell you how many people I know who were perfectly happy together until they got married, and then—wham."

"Why bother? Nobody has to get married nowadays, you know."

"Do you know what the statistical chances are of a marriage lasting?"

"Are you expecting?"

"I suppose you got tired of looking."

"Are you sure you know what you're doing?"

"I hope you've got a good lawyer."

"I hope you're keeping your apartment."

"Yeah, I thought I was going to live happily ever after, too."

"People change after they get married."

"Are you having a big wedding? Let me tell you, that is a nightmare."

"Aren't you having a big wedding? Let me tell you, you'll always regret not having had one."

Pregnancy also used to inspire congratulations. But now it's:

"Did you mean to get pregnant?"

"Oh yes, having babies is a big trend now."

"Do you think it's right to bring a child into today's world?"

"Do you know what tuition will be by the time this child goes to school?"

"Have you had all those tests to make sure there aren't any defects?"

"It's a shame to tie yourself down while you're still so young."

"It's not fair to give children older parents."

"I had the most awful time when I was pregnant."

"Let me tell you about my delivery."

"What's this going to do to your career?"

"Babies break up a lot of marriages."

"No matter what you do, you'll never get your figure back."

"Isn't your doctor worried about how much (how little) weight you've gained?"

"I suppose you're trying for a boy (girl)?"

"For God's sake, don't you know that's bad for the baby?"

"The people at work are really going to resent this."

"Don't you think there are enough people in the world?"

"You can still do something about it, you know."

When the baby arrives, there is another opportunity to avoid congratulations:

"Enjoy them while you can—it won't be long before they hate you."

"Don't you feel guilty about working (not working)?"

"People who have children get so boring."

"Watch out when your husband gets jealous of the baby."

"Your wife won't be interested in you anymore."

The noncongratulatory words offered to a new graduate include:

"Okay, you have a diploma, but do you have any useful skills?"

"You can get credit for just about anything in school nowadays."

"Your parents must be relieved you're off their dole now."

"Now you'll find out what it's really like out there."

"I've heard the job market is the worst it's ever been."

The work cycle has also been cleared of congratulations. For a job promotion, the message is:

"Of course you got it—you're (choose one: black, a woman, Hispanic, a member of the Old Boy Network)."

"I suppose you'll drop all your old friends now."

"Your spouse is going to resent this—they all do."

For a retirement:

"That's when you start going downhill fast; I've seen it happen."

"You're going to find that all your friends forget you."

"You'll be bored to tears."

"Your spouse is going to hate having you around all the time."

Miss Manners understands that in comparison with all these emotionally charged statements, merely telling people you are sad or happy for them—preferably sad because they are, and happy because they are, rather than the other way around—seems tame.

In compensation, she would like to point out that saying **"Congratulations"** or **"I'm so sorry,"** as the case may be, should relieve what many people describe as a burden. The biggest excuse for ignoring the big events in other people's lives is, as those not familiar with etiquette freely tell her, not knowing what to say.

The solutions that occur to them are: sharing their experiences of the same event, warning others what can go wrong, and advising others on what their attitude should be toward what has happened.

None of this needs doing. People who are getting married or having a baby are seldom suddenly seized with curiosity about the experiences of others in similar situations. If they are, they have no trouble asking. They feel it is their turn. *They're* getting married or *they're* having the baby. Why do they have to keep quiet while everyone else talks about having done these things in the past?

Warnings could only be useful to people who felt a lack of worries of their own, and would thus be grateful to be given some. Normal people find it upsetting to be invited to consider dreadful possibilities they cannot hope to avert.

People whose lives are being enriched often take the simple view that if life is good, one should be happy—and the outrageous view that their friends should be happy for them. They would enjoy hearing their friends say so, in those highly conventional ways.

RESTRAINT

DEAR MISS MANNERS—I am at an age when many of my friends are getting married. Most of the time, I genuinely congratulate them. But what do I say to those couples who seem to bring out the worst in each other? Who argue, break up and get back together forty times before deciding that marriage will solve their problems? Is the engagement the proper time to "speak now, or forever hold your peace"? I'm a person who finds it almost impossible not to convey my feelings, regardless of what I verbalize.

GENTLE READER—Miss Manners is afraid that you are dangerously mistaken about the intention of that line you quote from the marriage service. It is not the signal for self-appointed marriage counselors to predict incompatibility.

The words you are searching for are: **"I hope you'll both be very happy."** This must be said heartily, as if you believe there is a possibility they may be. What is more, there is; outsiders are notorious for failing to fathom whether or not marriages will work.

Miss Manners is aware that her advice goes against your declaration that you find it impossible not to convey your feelings regardless, apparently, of the consequences to other people's feelings. She believes this would be a good time to learn the survival skill of restraint.

ENCOURAGING RESTRAINT

DEAR MISS MANNERS—Upon hearing the news of my engagement to a wonderfully caring, intelligent creative man, several of my friends commented disparagingly on the length of our six-month courtship and advised me to reconsider. While I sincerely appreciate their concern for my welfare, I am comfortable with my decision and glad to have found such a loving man to spend my life with.

However well-intentioned my friends' comments, they have somewhat lessened my joy in my upcoming wedding. I would rather enjoy this special time with their support, not their censure. Is there a polite way to discourage such comments, while assuring my friends that I value and appreciate the motive for their concern?

GENTLE READER—How the idea got around that announcing an engagement amounts to calling for a referendum on the proposed marriage, Miss Manners does not know. But an awful lot of people seem to think that their opinions, rather than their good wishes, are required.

Miss Manners is afraid that you will have to prompt them to say **"I wish you the best"** (to you as a bride) or **"Congratulations"** (to the bridegroom, who is presumed to be the more fortunate of the pair) instead of *"Do you know what you're doing?"*

Whenever you have something nice to tell people—the fact of your engagement, or a pleasant detail, such as that you have found a wedding dress, or have been warmly received by his family—preface it by saying, **"You're such a dear friend—I know you'll be happy for me."** It is difficult for a well-intentioned person to deny this statement.

If a few determined ones persist, you too must persist. This may lead to some bizarre exchanges:

"But how do you know he isn't an ax-murderer?"

"Oh, I knew you'd be happy for me—isn't he wonderful?"

Eventually, however, it should help produce more of a bridal atmosphere.

THE UNEXPECTED REPLY

DEAR MISS MANNERS—I asked a young woman I worked with how she and her husband were. She married about a year ago, and I know the man, as well.

She informed me she was getting divorced. Her reply was clearly bitter and angry. I fell silent after that and went back to work. Silence seemed wrong, but I couldn't think what would be right to say considering how upset she was.

GENTLE READER—The lady is not excused, on the grounds of personal pain, for the rudeness of treating a conventional politeness as an affront. Miss Manners would have murmured quietly, **"I hope you'll each be very happy,"** and returned, as you did, to work.

THE MODEST REPLY

DEAR MISS MANNERS—You have said that one does not drink a toast to oneself. How does one behave, then, both when the assembled pause with their glasses waiting for one to join in the toast, and when one wants to acknowledge the good feelings of one's friends?

GENTLE READER—Do you mean if they all stand there with their glasses, looking foolish, as if you are supposed to lead the drinking in your own honor? That's a tough choice you're giving Miss Manners: between appearing vainglorious or ungracious. Let's see if we can avoid both.

Give them a minute, smiling modestly, hands to your sides. If no one makes a move, lift your glass, say **"And I want to drink to my dear friends"** and drink the second toast while they get started on the first.

CORRECT FUSSING

Baby-fussing (in the sense of fussing over babies, as opposed to what babies do when they want to observe parents going over the brink) is a classic example of the social contract: I'll admire your baby if you admire mine.

This is your basic Kitchy-Kitchy-Koo Deal. Miss Manners would not have thought it a difficult bargain to understand. The principle of mutuality on which it is based is also the one on which the entire concept of civilization is based. While it is true that babies couldn't care less what people think of their beauty or charm (an attitude that would be a severe impediment to civilization if it were allowed to flourish), parents require admiration for what they have produced, and therefore the society must provide it.

Yet the job is not being done as it should be. Instead of admiring other people's babies, those who are old enough to know better are taking the opportunity to critique the babies they meet:

"He's kind of small, isn't he?"

"You can probably get her ears flattened back when she's older."

"Is that a birthmark? Will it come off?"

Or they will use the occasion to attempt to satisfy their curiosity about where babies come from:

"Were you intending to have a baby, or did this just happen?"

In regard to multiple births or adoptions, the questions get ever more specific:

"Were you on fertility drugs?" "Did you have artificial insemination?" "How long had you been trying?"

"Where'd you get him?"

"Do you know anything about his real parents?"

"Why didn't they want him?"

"How long did you try before you gave up?"

"Don't you know that it's all a matter of not being tense, and now you'll be able to have your own children?"

"How can you be sure she doesn't have some kind of hereditary disease?"

All of these remarks understandably infuriate parents, who were expecting something more along the lines of **"Awwwww."** Since infuriating the custodians of our future is not a useful function, Miss Manners has to ask herself why it is going on.

One reason has to do with a literal interpretation of mutuality. Those who do not have children, or do not have them yet, or had them long ago, do not seem to feel that the bargain applies to them.

Yes, it does. Miss Manners should not have to remind people of such basic facts of life as sudden surges of nature among former child-loathers, or as a result of the appearance of grandchildren.

Even in the absence of any possibility of either, everyone is required to fuss over babies, just as everyone is required to pay taxes to support the school system. This is tribute we pay to the future, in the hope that it will contain such things as young geriatric specialists after our own nice old doctors have passed on.

Another reason has to do with a more widespread social disaster, which is the belief that admiration has to be genuine. Oddly enough, parents do not want frank assessments of their babies, much less frank inquiries into their provenance.

What do they want? Perhaps ignorance on that point is the problem. We are at the sad stage, Miss Manners has come to realize, where polite conventions have been ignored so long that even kindly disposed people no longer know what they are. In regard to babies, the rules are that all observations must be flattering, and all inquiries devoid of general interest.

Thus, **"My, what a beautiful baby"** and **"Isn't she the most adorable thing you ever saw?"** are excellent remarks to make about any baby. There is no need to worry that the parents will suspect one is exaggerating.

If something more specific is required, either size or disposition may be mentioned—but not any size or disposition. For reasons Miss Manners has never quite understood, babies are valued by the pound, so a polite remark would be how big and robust the baby is. For small babies, one says, **"Look what long fingers he has!"**—although long eyelashes will do as well.

Cooing babies do not present a problem, but what about those who are crying or asleep? Of the former, one can say, **"She's so alert!"** and of the latter, **"Look how angelic he is."**

A proper inquiry is, **"How old is she?"** although nowadays people do not seem to know when such a question is no longer appropriate. Miss Manners has heard it asked of 40-year-olds.

Any question beginning with *"Does he . . ."* and containing the word *"yet"* is improper. Unlike the rest of the population, babies do not have to "do" anything to be admired, although calling attention to minimal achievements is permissible: **"Oh, look! She's looking back at me!"**

It should not be a matter of concern that all this does not add up to much conversationally. Neither parent nor child will feel the lack.

INCORRECT FUSSING

DEAR MISS MANNERS—To our delight, my husband and I are expecting our fourth child. We have yet to share this news with anyone, as it seems that in our society, the politically correct number of children is two. (Exceptions are made only if your first two children happen to be of the same sex.)

As with my third pregnancy, I'm anticipating some snide, rude and nosy questions from friends, acquaintances, relatives and strangers. Everyone seems to be so full of "wisdom"! How should I reply to phony pity, personal questions about my birth control practices or comments on how this child must be a mistake?

Other stupid remarks I've heard are, *"I'm glad it's you and not me!"* and the ever-clever *"You do know how babies are made, don't you?"*

Someone even dared to quiz us on our finances! We have worked hard to provide a good home where children are welcome and loved. I don't care if I ever take a trip abroad, wear a three-carat diamond ring or drive a sport car. These things don't matter to me. But some of my friends and family will surely be scandalized at my latest accomplishment, which will not be a secret much longer.

GENTLE READER—One of the joys of being a parent is that it gives one a lot of practice in dealing with foolishness.

As you might with an out-of-line child, stare these people down, ignore their attempts to get to you and remain firmly polite. By refusing to respond to their outrages and saying instead, **"I'm sure you mean to wish us the best,"** you could even teach them something. Such as that the correct thing to say when someone is expecting a first or eleventh baby is **"Congratulations."**

Miss Manners agrees that it is a shame you have to use this valuable technique on adults who should have been socialized by their own parents to avoid nosiness, crude teasing and other rudeness. But at least you know how to do it.

SYMPATHY

Bad people take off like a shot when their friends suffer illness or failure, lose their jobs or lose their relatives. The good stick around and visit the unfortunate, offering them the benefit of their sympathy and wisdom. And making them feel worse.

Miss Manners hastens to say that it is not the fact of friends sticking around that troubles people at the low points of their lives. It is a duty of mercy to do so and generally people are appropriately grateful to those who stand by them when they are in trouble. What gets to them is the sympathy and wisdom that those friends feel compelled to offer.

Rather than say the simple, perhaps even banal, but deeply touching thing that etiquette requires—**"I hope you know how much I care and that you can count on me"**—most people feel obliged to come up with something more elaborate. Here are some currently popular styles in comforting the downtrodden, who are apparently not yet miserable enough.

1. *Things Could Be Worse.*
Rather than deal with the tragedy that actually has occurred, the person who favors this approach recites to the victim all the things that didn't occur, and then offers congratulations that they didn't. If you broke your leg, you are fortunate that it wasn't your arm. If you lost a parent, you are fortunate that it wasn't your child. If your house burned down, you are fortunate that it was insured. If you got mugged, you are fortunate that you didn't get killed. And so on. There is a clear suggestion that you ought to be rejoicing instead of moping.

2. You Think You Have Troubles?

This is a more personal variation of the previous technique. It offers a competition that the candidate for comfort is bound to lose, to show the victim that other acquaintances of the comforter's should be the center of sympathetic attention, not the person with the immediate problem.

It is characterized by the phrase *"that's nothing."* You had an automobile accident? That's nothing. A friend of mine was in a plane that nearly crashed on take-off. Your husband asked for a trial separation? That's nothing. I know someone whose husband has a contract out to have her killed. Here the sufferer is accused of being selfish for dwelling on his or her own troubles instead of worrying about unknown others who are more deserving of sympathy.

3. It's All for the Best.

This is not an attempt to deny the importance of the tragedy, only to redefine it as a gain. The key phrase is *"better off."* The person who died is better off no longer suffering and the survivors are better off because they no longer have to offer care or worry. Your son's murderer has been convicted and you are better off because now you can achieve closure. You are better off that your car was stolen because you probably would have had to trade it in soon anyway and this way you get the insurance. You are better off not getting promoted because there would have been so much more work. This also suggests that the victim is ungrateful to feel bad when everything is actually going very well.

4. It's All Your Fault.

This technique does away with the phony optimism and the pretense that there shouldn't be any bad feelings. On the contrary, feeling sorry about your fate isn't enough; you should feel guilty. The line of comfort is *"Well, what did you expect?"* Of course, you had a heart attack. You were eating all that heavy food. What did you expect? Of course your property was vandalized. You didn't have an alarm system. What did you expect? Of course your son got shot. He was in the wrong place at the wrong time. What did you expect? The comfort that is being offered here is that justice is being done.

5. Go Ahead and Feel Terrible.

This may be Miss Manners' all-time favorite, because it attacks the person who is coping well with tragedy, even if only doing so momentarily, and encourages a display of misery. You don't have to keep up a brave front with me. You look terrible. You've got to start working through your grief. Give yourself permission to cry. Come on, don't try to kid me, I know you're miserable. This is the comfort that says I know you're unhappy, but you're not unhappy enough. What are friends for?

INSULTING SYMPATHY

DEAR MISS MANNERS—I will be out in public, in my wheelchair, with my arm, back and leg braces, when someone, nearly always a woman, will make a point of coming over to speak with me. First, this person will say that seeing me made her feel so much better. Then she will go on to say it is because she felt she was in such terrible physical condition until she saw me.

I need to memorize some response because, frankly, I am too confused to answer at first and once I find words, they are generally not appropriate for either polite or educational conversation and so are left unsaid. I have stared in amazement or simply said, "Thank you," but my best friend tells me that these replies are not adequate to the situation. I desire to avoid pity and awkward public situations, but I desire to maintain my emotional equilibrium.

GENTLE READER—**"Thank you"** strikes Miss Manners as a very good reply, in that it is itself polite and yet ought to make anyone with a shred of decency realize the enormity of the insult in remarks that are also disguised as thanks.

If that doesn't work, we shall just have to step it up a bit. Add, in the kindest of tones, **"You know, I too feel so much better off now that I have observed you."**

Unfortunately, the full impact of this remark does not hit until the person has had a chance to think it over. But although you will not be there to see it—probably in the middle of the night such a person realizes that you have favorably compared yourself with her—Miss Manners promises it will happen.

CHAPTER 2

EVERYDAY CONVENTIONS

EUPHEMISM

Etiquette has a reputation for mincing words. Miss Manners is not sure what is wrong with this interesting procedure. But it must be a great sin, because it is always described in the negative and with great pride, as in, *"I NEVER mince words."*

It seems to Miss Manners that there are times when words need to be minced. Not everyone wants to hear—or to volunteer—information in such a vivid way as to create mental pictures that are not likely to agree with other people's lunches.

Euphemisms are much maligned these days. Using one invites a charge of (we need some loud, ominous music here) *NOT BEING WILLING TO FACE THE TRUTH.* Of course, if no one understood the truth behind these circumlocutions, the delicacy that prompts them would defeat itself. The idea is to convey the information, but without rubbing people's faces in it. Such restraint seems to upset people.

Two Gentle Readers who give their ages (and thus put themselves in a category Miss Manners would describe as elderly, were she not afraid of offending them by not being blunt enough to say something such as "whose lives are at least three quarters over") report being bothered by the lack of frankness in modern society.

"When I was a child," writes one, "my parents, and, I

believe, my pediatrician, referred to body elimination as 'No. 1' and 'No. 2.' When I raised my children, the terms used by the pediatrician were urine and bowel movement. Now I am appalled that my college-educated children, their friends, and their pediatricians use the terms 'pee' and 'poop.' Are other grandmothers as critical of this terminology as I am?"

Miss Manners hasn't polled the grandmother population, but she suspects that quite a few of them have been overexposed to even more succinct terms than those on which this lady reared her children. You have only to walk down the street nowadays, to hear someone use an expression that is certainly not "Oh, poop!"

Admittedly, the words to which the Gentle Reader objects are on the cute side for medical usage. But since few children have been taught to adjust their vocabulary to the social context, Miss Manners thinks it just as well for their doctors not to insist upon words that do not suit every occasion.

Another Gentle Reader declares that "when I was younger, people were called 'divorced,' 'widowed,' 'single' or 'unwed mother'" and objects that "nowadays, everyone is called single."

Miss Manners recalls this usage somewhat differently. Ladies were called divorcées, widows, unwed mothers or spinsters; gentlemen not currently married, with or without progeny, were all called bachelors. Miss Manners finds the simple, evenly applied, none-of-your-business-why term for everyone to be a decided improvement.

Not all changes are for the better, certainly. Here are some less fortunate instances of alterations of conventional expressions that Miss Manners' Gentle Readers have reported:

"If I say something in all seriousness, and it is truthful, the reply is always, *'You're kidding.'*" (The proper expression to a surprising announcement is **"Oh, really?"**)

"Why are businesses now directing their receptionists, when taking a caller's name, to ask, *'How are you spelling that?'* I'm tempted to answer, 'Oh, this week I'm adding an extra letter just to confuse 'em.' What's wrong with 'How do you spell that?' or **'Would you spell your name, please?'** " (What, indeed?)

"People who give directions or answer questions now correct the inquirer with a haughtily sharp staccato *'No-na-NO!'* as in 'Will you be open tomorrow till 11 p.m.?' 'No-na-NO! Tomorrow till 9; Tuesday and Thursday till 11.'" (Three words are required, but "no" is only one of them. The others are **"I'm sorry."**)

"The answer to 'Would you care for anything else?' at the dinner table, now seems to be *'I'm so full'* or *'I'm stuffed'* or *'I'm ready to pop.'* This implies that they are gluttonous and ill mannered in expressing their discomfort to those at the table." (The correct way to decline an offer of food or drink is still **"No, thank you,"** not these charming threats to burst, nor even the more dainty *"I'm fine"* one hears so often now.)

"As a response to 'Thank you,' I have a problem with *'No problem'* because it introduces the idea that there in fact is a problem, and that the person has graciously decided to overlook it." (The answer to "Thank you" is still **"You're welcome,"** despite the Gentle Reader who was kind enough to look up "welcome" in the dictionary and, finding that it signified a cordial reception, pleaded for the more British "My pleasure." It is not even the kindly meant *"Thank YOU."* And it certainly isn't *"No sweat."* Nor is it *"Quite all right,"* which is slightly cold, suggesting that one was thanked for something one would rather not have done.

"PLEASE"

DEAR MISS MANNERS—What seems to be a fast-growing practice threatens (in my humble opinion) the very core of human civility. It is the use of the phrase *"I need you to . . ."* in place of the word **"please."**

I first noticed this rude manner of request at my work place. Well, I thought, perhaps some company-run management workshop had suggested using this sad phrase as a means of clearly stating an order, as opposed to a request, to get things done. This half-hearted rationalization allowed me to shrug it off for a time. More recently, however, I am hearing it directed at customers by salespeople! "I need you to sign here," they say. And "I'll need you to take that receipt over to register four."

Miss Manners, what on earth can they be thinking? I do not pretend to be anything close to a symbol of gentility and good taste. My background is humble, and my career with a delivery company did not keep me surrounded by high society. But I cannot recall even one occasion when my poor parents said "I need you to pass the potatoes," or when any of my teachers back in the Bronx "needed me" to clean the chalk board. They said "please" and "thank you" just as my wife and children and I still do (with good results) today.

GENTLE READER—Miss Manners is extremely grateful for that. What is more, she knows how to thank you. You draw to her attention an interesting development (as we say in the etiquette business to designate a loathsome deterioration). She tries not to get worked up into a froth over sloppy new phrases, because it would preclude her ever getting to anything else—but the omission of the word "please" is a serious matter.

"EXCUSE ME"

DEAR MISS MANNERS—What, if anything, do you say after a person burps and then says **"Excuse me"**? I always feel awkward. Do you say *"Hey, no problem," "Any time," "You're forgiven,"* or do you just not say anything at all? I would rather say something.

GENTLE READER—You seem seriously to have misinterpreted the depth of that brief form, "Excuse me," which courteously acknowledges a multitude of minor infractions. (But Miss Manners graciously forgives you. Any time.) "Excuse me" is not shorthand for "Good heavens, what have I done? Will you ever forgive me?" A closer colloquial equivalent would be "Whoops." No reply is appropriate.

INTRODUCTIONS

There are two basic forms in current use for performing social introductions, Miss Manners has observed.

The first, in its entirety, is *"This is my friend."* Variations include *"That's my mom, glaring at us"* and *"I figured you wouldn't mind if I brought someone."*

The second goes something like this: *"You two will love each other. Brittany has her own plant counseling service, and she's doing great. She visits plants while their owners are away and deals not just with water but with their inner needs; and now that you have a lover on the coast—didn't I tell you you'd find someone when you finally did something with your hair?— I imagine you're away a lot. I told her you live in that new area where houses start at a quarter of a million. She's a recovering alcoholic and her ex doesn't pay child support."*

In spite of the impressive simplicity of the first, and the

warm spirit of confidence of the second, these two methods of making strangers acquainted have more in common with each other than with any traditional form. Both manage to conceal who is being introduced, let alone how either is to be addressed by a new acquaintance. Neither one serves to prompt polite conversation.

Oh, Miss Manners supposes that the socially adept will manage. They can open with *"Hi, Mom!"* or *"Sure, come on in, that's the third time this month you've shown up with someone new."* Or they can just plunge into conversation by saying, *"I know someone you can hire to track down your ex-husband and throw him in jail if he doesn't pay up,"* or *"Boy, people will pay for anything nowadays,"* or *"I gather you're loaded"* or *"I hope you and that new lover are being really careful."*

No wonder no one wants to bother with learning how to perform the old proper introduction. You can have too much excitement with these new ones. Nevertheless, Miss Manners believes it might be useful to acquire the skill of supplying the proper amount of information, but not so much that those being introduced will have nothing further to learn from each other.

Even when the simple form was well known (**"Mrs. Twaddle, may I present Mr. Whiffle?"**) people used to fret terribly about who was supposed to be introduced to whom. They knew, of course, that:

- a gentleman is presented to a lady
- a low-ranking person to a higher one
- a younger one to an elder
- a relative to an acquaintance

But real life, not being so simple, kept the etiquette business alert with an endless supply of examples in which these rules were in riotous conflict.

Sample question: How do you introduce a young minister who is also in the state senate, and an elderly female sinner who is also a duchess?

Answer: Don't worry, they already know each other.

Nowadays, however, it's back to the boring basics. Miss Manners would be happy if she could just get across the difficult point that it is necessary, when making people acquainted, to say their names. (You may not know their names of course, but that is another problem, and not a new one. Proper people are as likely as anyone else to get addled, some would say more so, and etiquette is full of tricks to make people come up with their own names when supposedly being introduced. Such as **"It's not possible that the two most interesting people I know don't already know each other—whoops, I'll be right back."**)

What is more, even now, respectable people have a minimum of two names. Both should be used. Introductions by first names only make your friends sound as if they have a reason for concealing their identities, as well as making it difficult for them to pursue further acquaintance without doing potentially embarrassing or difficult research. ("Which Daniel do you want—the one who used to room with David, or the one who lives down the block or that great guy I just met myself—and by the way, what do you have in mind?")

What is not necessary is to give each person's professional credentials. It is so common now to state occupations in situations that have, or should have, nothing to do with business that Miss Manners should probably save her breath instead of protesting. Nevertheless, you should be aware that half the people hate this practice because they don't feel they sound important enough and the other half hate it because they want to be loved for themselves.

As for personal information—*"I wanted you two to meet, because you're both single"*—that's only if you hate them both, and even then it should be resisted. Full names and a passing fact—**"Tatiana's just back from skiing," "Brian organized the walkathon last week"**—should be enough to get people off to a good start, even if it is to say, when you've gone, "I've never skied in my life, it was golf," and "That's okay, my name's not Brian, it's Brad."

There is also the issue of when and whether to introduce people at all. Miss Manners uses the Standing Around Feeling Stupid test in these matters. If someone is likely to be left standing around long enough to feel stupid during an encounter with a third person, introductions are in order.

"HOW ARE YOU?"

DEAR MISS MANNERS—I find it especially annoying when someone I don't know calls on the phone (as one did last week for a political poll) and asks, "How are you?" in response to my "Hello." People ask "How are you?" when we pass in the supermarket aisle, or when we are seated next to each other in a doctor's office.

I realize that this is a semi-rhetorical question, but it seems to demand a "Fine, thank you, and how are you?" Perhaps I am a little paranoid, but at times this question seems to be a power play, as if the questioner might be forcing a reply to intimidate, especially if it is on a dark street or in a parking deck.

Am I rude to ask the phone caller to identify himself

before I blurt a reply? Am I obligated to answer this question at all? Wouldn't a "hello" or "hi" or "good morning" be much more comfortable, polite, and efficient? How about just a winning smile and a nod of acknowledgment?

GENTLE READER—The nuances of asking how people are, although correctly interpreted by most people, are so complex that Miss Manners feels like a fool having so much to say about so apparently simple a question.

"How are you?" (or, more likely, "How ya doin'?") may, depending on circumstances, be a ritual question requiring the ritual answer **"Very well, thank you, and you?"** (or "Jes' fine; how're you?"), or it may be a literal question requiring a more or less literal (let's not be too graphic) answer.

On the telephone the answerer supplies the greeting of **"Hello,"** but the caller is required to supply immediate identification. Anyone who tries, instead, to begin a conversation anonymously (except your mother, who can't understand why you don't recognize her voice) is up to no good. So your response should be a crisp reminder: **"Who is this, please?"**

Real friends with time to spare may be asking how you are out of a desire to know. But even solicitude should not be abused: A two-sentence reply is quite enough, with the implication that further details are available upon request.

In contrast, two people passing in a supermarket aisle would be merely exchanging the question ritually, unless they intended to block the aisle and hold a conversation. Two people who pass in the dark should be following the ritual of keeping their distance silently.

In the doctor's waiting room, the question could be either a mere acknowledgment of the other person's presence, in which case the ritual response of "Fine, etc." is required (however at variance that may be with the obvious fact of waiting to see a doctor) or, if accompanied by a serious look, it could be an invitation to exchange symptoms.

Silly as these overlapping possibilities may seem, they are highly useful, and you will find that you know most of them without having to think about this matter. Miss Manners only needs to assure you that when someone asks how you are out of an obvious and unwelcome attempt to probe your state of being, you may retreat into the conventional **"Fine, thank you,"** as a polite way of omitting mention of your bankruptcy, divorce and rebelling intestines.

Things get even more complicated when you realize that **"How do you do?"** is not considered to be a question. It is a greeting, to which the proper answer is **"How do you do?"** Saying "How do you do?" is a ritual. It might help to think of it as the original answer-a-question-with-a-question.

Don't think you're going to beat Miss Manners down by pointing out to her that this doesn't make any sense; lots of the little folk customs we call etiquette do not. Nor does etiquette pretend to be consistent. Right after saying that "How do you do?" is not intended to be interpreted literally, it decrees that *"I'm pleased to meet you"* is an improper answer because it is impossible to know in advance if there will be pleasure in the association.

"YOU LOOK TERRIBLE"

DEAR MISS MANNERS—What is the correct response to someone who greets you by saying you look tired, when you yourself didn't feel tired, or when you had thought that in fact you looked quite well? A response that would also discourage similar opening remarks in the future would be particularly useful, as this type of "concerned" comment can have a rather negative effect on a person who might otherwise be feeling fine and having a perfectly reasonable day.

GENTLE READER—**"Oh, dear, how discouraging. I was feeling so chipper before you said that."**

"I'VE HEARD ABOUT YOU"

DEAR MISS MANNERS—I am often unnerved when someone is introduced to me and says, *"Oh, I've heard so much about you."* Am I being unduly suspicious? Insecure? Oversensitive? After all, what kind of person would want you to speculate whether he or she is privy to several juicy bits of gossip about you?

Still, the line is frequently stated so ambiguously that I find it difficult to assume that what the person heard was flattering, or even positive. I never use the phrase myself unless I can remove any doubt by inquiring about at least one heroic act, display of kindness or witty statement. How do I respond? I've read your column long enough to know that it is unacceptable to say, *"You'll never guess what I heard about you."*

GENTLE READER—Miss Manners doesn't want to appear to be unduly suspicious either. But she is dying to know what there is to know about you that you are afraid might be getting around. The rest of us egotists take it for granted that this statement means "I've been told how wonderful you are."

To assume that the briefing included specific evidence of that wonder, such as you graciously volunteer when you meet someone, is perhaps exaggerated. The usual preparation is probably more like "She's very nice; you'll like her." To assume that anyone would hint at having received an unfavorable report also seems exaggerated. Such warnings are usually a matter of secrecy.

Just in case you do have reason to believe that there are wild rumors circulating about you, Miss Manners gives you leave to respond cheerfully, **"Well, it's all true."** That is especially the thing to say if it is true. The surest way to spread unpleasant gossip about yourself is to go around denying it. Otherwise, the polite reply is, **"Belinda speaks highly of you too."**

DAILY GREETINGS

A radio program of Miss Manners' acquaintance has been asked why the announcer begins the broadcast by saying **"Good morning,"** when the news that follows is so often bad. Presumably, it would be more fitting to address those who have set their radio-alarms for the early morning news by shouting "Wake up! A lot of people are dead!"

A telephone operator who was handling a call for Miss Manners asked timidly, "Would you mind if I wished you a nice day?" Clearly, past experience had taught her that she was in danger of being verbally abused by anyone on whom she perpetrated such a wish without express permission.

Miss Manners wishes these people would have the goodness to refrain from removing small politenesses from the pleasant habit of daily greetings, and from discouraging others from the habit of using them. Or, as she might say if she shared their own desire for direct talk that conveys emotions in keeping with the sentiment expressed, *"Yo! Shut up!"*

Miss Manners does not talk that way. She is not even tempted to do so. In no household of which she has been a part was the phrase *"shut up"* ever permitted, other than in regard to what one had to do to the house before leaving for the summer holiday.

The untouched-up response to this statement is undoubtedly **"Oh, good for you."** Miss Manners would therefore like to explain why her standard is, indeed, good for her, and for everyone else. It is her contention that blunt greetings, not pleasant ones, are dishonest and misleading.

To understand her argument, you must have a modicum of sophistication. (How's that for plain speaking?) You must realize that language conveys more than the literal meaning of each word. To begin with, "Good morning" is not an elliptical version of "It is a good morning," but of "I wish you a good morning." It does not refer specifically to weather or news, but leaves open the possibility of any sort of good fortune.

So, of course, does the current and much attacked remark (used in parting, rather than greeting) "Have a nice day." Those who snarl back "I don't want to have a nice day" are being illogical, as the vague word niceness is used to refer to whatever it is that they do wish.

However, what all of this amounts to is the overinterpretation of the habits of politeness. What these phrases really convey is that the person who pronounces them is not looking for a fight. Wishing someone well is the normal conventional posture; those who have ill wishes to convey must specifically articulate them. Miss Manners only wishes they would confine themselves to confronting one another and leave the rest of us unchallenged in our hopes of having some nice days.

"GOOD DAY"

DEAR MISS MANNERS—I was reading the secretary's manual at work, and it said that the secretary should greet visitors with **"Good morning"** or **"Good afternoon."** But I have heard that "Good afternoon" is a term of dismissal and should not be used as a greeting.

GENTLE READER—No, no, it is **"Good day"** that has become a declaration of polite dismissal. Miss Manners acknowledges that **"Good afternoon"** could also serve the purpose, if stated in a firm enough tone of voice (those without firmness are advised to stand up, perhaps even to march to the door and stand by it). Pleasantly spoken, however, it still serves as a greeting.

CONCLUDING CONVERSATION

DEAR MISS MANNERS—What should one do when a friend or acquaintance calls on the phone and then does not take responsibility for carrying the conversation? Several times I have had someone call me, and then stay on the line with nothing to say—thus there is a silence, which makes me uncomfortable—but does not end the call.

I usually end up saying something like, "Well, I'll be going now," or "I guess I'll talk to you later." I feel incorrect, though, because I wonder if it is my place to end the call since I did not initiate it.

GENTLE READER—You are correct in believing that the person who made the telephone call should be the one to end it, just as a guest who shows up in person should be the one to end the visit. But, as your experience attests, one could die waiting.

The polite solution is a skill known as Speeding the Parting Guest. Miss Manners is delighted to report that there is a popular new expression designed precisely for doing so on the telephone. The phrase is **"Well, I won't keep you."** It has the polite advantage of seeming to worry about intruding, rather than being intruded on, and is thus an improvement on such previous expressions as you mention, or the various versions of **"I think I hear my mother calling me."**

CONCLUDING A VISIT

DEAR MISS MANNERS—I was wondering what is the proper way to say good-bye. Sometimes I feel compelled to say something witty or pithy, but I feel very awkward saying it. I am always afraid that I will not come off as enthusiastic about a host's party or gathering if I do not say something amazing, but somehow it never works.

GENTLE READER—Of course it doesn't work. After a long day preparing to entertain you, and a full evening doing so, however delightful it may have been, these people do not want to be amazed.

They want to be thanked, after which they want to be allowed to do the dishes and/or go to bed. But they are frozen at the doorstep while you try to top off the evening with some piece of repartee everybody is too tired to appreciate.

Originality is not everything. The words hosts most want to hear when the evening is over are **"Thank you, I had a wonderful time"** and **"Good night."**

CHAPTER 3

SAYING "NO" AND OTHER NEGATIVE NICETIES

REJECTION

Here is one of etiquette's paradoxes: When one person offers another a chunk of his or her innermost soul, especially when the plea is accompanied by a beseeching look and a lot of talk about feelings, it seems not quite nice to refuse. Yet we all know about people who never refuse such offers, and "nice" is the last word generally used to describe them.

Miss Manners tries not to be so harsh. Ever gratified by evidence of sensitivity to causing pain, she believes that the trouble with a girl who can't say no must be an excess of good-heartedness. She wishes to relieve such do-gooders of their burden by explaining how to soften rejections so as to produce a minimum of anguish.

Notice that Miss Manners dares to use the dreaded word "rejection." In a society where insults are called communication, and selfishness proclaims itself to be self-esteem, the timidity about being responsible for rejections is astonishing. Miss Manners is forever hearing from exasperated ladies or gentlemen who want to know the approved technique for getting rid of someone "without," they hasten to add, making that person "feel rejected."

She hates to have to point out that a person who doesn't feel rejected doesn't go away. A painless rejection isn't one.

Notice, also, that the issue Miss Manners proposes to discuss has to do with the soul. This may include not only offers of love, but of such emotion-laden efforts as creative work. What it does not include is heartless offers, no matter how much of the rest of the body is thrown in. Far from cautioning against rejecting that kind of proposal, etiquette advises doing so summarily.

"How dare you suggest such a thing!" was the traditional phrase. It was considered safer than "What do you take me for?" which might inspire a reply. (Miss Manners recognizes that most people now have trouble summoning surprise, if not indignation, in these cases, which is why the unadorned, unexplained—and certainly unapologetic—**"No"** is considered sufficiently honorable today.)

But what of the pathetic person timorously offering a heart-and-soul to an unrequiting heart-and-soul, or, worse, a poem to an editor?

Miss Manners is all for mercy toward those in such a tender state, provided this does not disguise the rejection so as to give false hope. The form that usually springs to the mind of the beseeched one— *"You must be kidding!"*—is not polite.

In the business world, the standard rejection is **"Thank you for thinking of us, but this does not suit our needs at the moment."** Miss Manners wishes to point out the valuable purpose served here by euphemism. How much pleasanter it is to have the necessity for rejection attributed to vague circumstances rather than documented personal inadequacies.

This professional form is so set, and so well understood, that the truly kind functionary will add a grace note— perhaps a handwritten **"But I enjoyed your idea"** or **"I hope you'll try us another time."**

Advice about failings that can be corrected—**"This**

might be acceptable if it were cut in half," "We might be interested when you finish your degree"—is, of course, correct and even generous. Not every organization is equipped for such tasks, however, and Miss Manners regrets to say that those who make unsolicited appeals have no cause for indignation when little or no time is devoted to answering them.

In personal life, the rules are different. No honorable offer can be ignored, and any version of "not now" seems like an invitation to try again.

Worst of all is so-called constructive criticism. The itemized lists in personal columns notwithstanding, love has very little to do with qualifications, and the person who advises a rejected suitor to get a better job, for example, is bound to fall in love with the next ne'er-do-well who comes along.

There is, however, an acceptable convention for personal rejections: **"I value you as a friend."** Everyone understands that that is the kiss of death of romance. As with the business form, dressing it up with whatever is plausible—**"I think you're a wonderful person," "I'm incredibly honored by your offer"**—is graceful without being misleading about the verdict.

It is not only out of pity that Miss Manners advises using versions of these standard forms, which are both gentle and clear. This is also to protect the rejecter. While Miss Manners discounts the protestations of those who announce "I can't take rejection" (when they only mean that they, like everyone else in the world, don't like it, but will jolly well take it if they have to), she promises that the memory of rejection is unusually durable. Later, when the rejected person has achieved spectacular success and tells the story of your rejection to adoring and incredulous admirers, it will be to your advantage to have your statement sound bland, routine and unoriginal.

BEING BUSY

DEAR MISS MANNERS How do you end a friendship with someone who refuses to take the hint?

Seven years ago, I had a year-long friendship (no dating) with a man with whom I had a few lunches and dinners and many long conversations. I became his dear friend—in his eyes. He was an odd hard-luck case who I felt rather sorry for, and he began to make me very uncomfortable. So I began making excuses about not seeing him, wouldn't take his calls at the office, and ended the conversation quickly when he did reach me.

That was six years ago, and he still calls. If I had dated him, I could say "It's best we don't speak," but we never dated. Is it polite to say "Don't call me any more," and is there some excuse I can use to make it less painful for him?

GENTLE READER—Miss Manners too would like to be gentle with a hard-luck case who fancies he has a friend in a lady who has refused to see him for six years. She suggests that this impulse be weighed against the nuisance value involved.

How often does he call? If it is once or twice a year, Miss Manners suggests you allow him to continue in his illusion. If it is once a month, you might add to your usual refusal, **"You know, I lead such a busy life that it's rather hopeless to expect that we will be able to get together. But I appreciate your thinking of me."**

OVERDOING BUSYNESS

But, stop bragging about how busy you are.

Miss Manners does not mean to be pettish. It's just that the plea of being busy, which has been doing indispensable duty on the social front for many years, is now so over worked that it is about to drop of exhaustion.

"I'm so sorry, but I'm busy then" is the proper way to decline nearly every proffered engagement except possibly one to be married. (That offer is most gracefully declined with an accompanying statement declaring one's own unworthiness to accept; this is not necessary when declining to help friends paint their house.)

The conventional expression of being busy is correctly done in a tone that seems to add "to my eternal regret," and does not exclude the idea that only stern duty has kept one from complying with such a tempting request. It is never accompanied by documentation. Indeed, its value is its vagueness. If you don't say what you are busy doing, no one else can presume to judge its relative importance, or how long it will last. You may well want to be busy forever.

That is not at all the same thing as the detailed pleas of eternal busyness that are so tediously common nowadays. A simple invitation for a cup of tea, the decline of which is not likely to break anybody's heart, is likely to bring on a torrent:

"A cup of tea? You must be joking—I only wish I had time for a cup of tea. My desk is piled so high I can't see over it. I've had to work nights and weekends for as long as I can remember. And we just got back from vacation, and I've had to move all that stuff from one house to the other, with practically no help. And speaking of help, the nanny's no good, and we're going to have to go through the whole business of looking for someone

else. Neither of us has the time to do it, we're both so behind in everything. We've got all these people coming too. They're all such bores, but they're clients. And then the relatives will be descending on us. We never get to spend any time with the children, much less alone. Do you know how long it is since I've had a quiet cup of tea with anyone? Wait a minute, there's another call, and I have to take it."

Ringing off on someone to take another call, usually so rude, is probably a blessing in this case. What, after all, is the poor thwarted host to say?

Probably "Oh, excuse me. I never should have presumed to suggest encroaching on such valuable time." Or, more likely, "Oh, good for you," which is not nice, but understandable.

Recitals of exactly how busy one is usually carry a whiff of self-importance, which Miss Manners couldn't help putting into her example, with its references to jobs, subordinates and resources. Swaggering is, of course, impolite in itself.

Even without that element, the recital of one's busyness, especially when made in response to the offer of kindness, such as an invitation, is offensive. Complaining to sympathetic listeners, who are also allowed a turn at complaining, may be a blameless relief, but complaining as an excuse is insulting. Even made in a pitiful tone, describing humble tasks, such a tale cannot help but suggest a contrast to the life of the listener. Like the person who breaks into a line announcing "I'm in a hurry," it carries the suggestion, "but you can wait because you have nothing important to do."

Few people have no demands on their time; those who feel themselves to be in that position are perhaps deafening themselves to the call of good work which needs to be done in the world. And so, Miss Manners suspects, are those who have enough time to go around telling innocent people all the details of their schedules.

THINKING TWICE

DEAR MISS MANNERS—For a special treat, I took my son to a movie of his choice. We arrived early and chose good viewing seats—I always place him on the aisle, so he can see around "big folks." The theater was very crowded.

Just at the point of the movie beginning, a mother and her handicapped daughter arrived (she was using hand crutches and was, I assume, a victim of cerebral palsy). The mother asked if we would move down so the daughter could sit on the aisle. As I hesitated, she quickly spied two aisle seats closer to the screen.

Although I have considerable sympathy for the handicapped, this would have prevented my son from having a clear view. Shouldn't they have arranged to arrive early for choice seats?

GENTLE READER—First-come, first-served is a good rule, but Miss Manners trusts it is not the only one you wish to teach your son. If you have sympathy for those with problems, surely you wish him to develop this as well.

Don't you? Yes?

No, you just want him to be able to see.

Miss Manners sympathizes with this reasonable and maternal desire. But she begs you not to let it prompt you to demonstrate that one should only look after oneself and one's own. Let's see if we can manage both.

Suppose you were to respond to the parent and child by saying, **"Of course, let me see if perhaps someone else can**

spare an aisle seat for my son, who has trouble seeing otherwise."

What will happen, then, is that the other mother will say, **"Never mind, let me find another row,"** and that others who overhear the conversation will volunteer their seats.

You say no—that all others will stick to what they perceive as their rights, regardless of anyone else's more compelling needs? Only, Miss Manners maintains, if their own parents skipped the lesson she is urging you to teach.

DUCKING A REQUEST

DEAR MISS MANNERS—When a new mother is visiting people with her new baby, who should ask about holding the child? Should the mother ask if someone wants to, or should the person who would like to hold the baby ask? Is there a courteous reply when you do not wish someone to hold your baby?

GENTLE READER—While mothers and guests may all too vividly envision the possible physical consequences of such transfers, Miss Manners would like to draw attention to the social consequences.

"Would you like to hold my baby?" and "May I hold the baby?" are both difficult requests to decline. In neither case is *"Good heavens, no"* a polite response.

The reluctant guest can only protest "I'm not good with babies; let me admire her from here," trading reputation for comfort. But a reluctant mother who gently says **"Now is probably not a good time"** only seems all the more considerate. The best lap visiting is therefore done when it is the owner of the lap who issues the invitation.

DUCKING PAPER

DEAR MISS MANNERS—I am an English professor, and am burdened by those interested in, but unknowledgeable about, my studies. I regularly receive books, manuscripts and articles "to read." These are sometimes direly bad (a first, unpublished novel by an acquaintance, for instance). These are delivered to me, uninvited, with expectations that I will read them, presumably with enjoyment, because, of course, I "love to read."

Worse yet, there is pressure to read the item soon and return it with thanks, commentary, remarks or even corrections. Sometimes my relatives send their children over to have me "look over" their essays and schoolwork. I am then usually part of a last-ditch try to "fix" last-minute work; I am then expected to drop everything and spend my evening editing the uninvited piece.

Because I have no chance of ever reading everything that I actually do want to read, I want to avoid reading that which I have no interest in, even if it is a relative's favorite best-seller. May I simply hand back the unwanted item when it is set down on my desk or carried into my house? Must I keep it a while and then return it with feigned sorrow that time prevented my "getting to it"?

The latter method often results in the object being redelivered to my care. I don't mind occasionally helping out, but I prefer to have volunteered my efforts. I don't mind reading recommended literature, but I'd like to express interest in doing so before being "loaned" a copy.

GENTLE READER—Miss Manners doesn't just sympathize with you, she identifies with you. And it's not only because of the pile of things she promised to read, but because of the shared distaste for the noun "loan" used as a verb.

Nevertheless, she must interrogate you sternly. Are you quite sure that you never asked a lawyer-friend to look over the contract for your apartment, your plumber-friend to do something about the drip in your sink and one of those young pupil-friends to retrieve the journal article, due tomorrow, that you had accidentally erased from your computer? Asking relatives and friends for free professional advice and services is rude—unless it is really mutual. At the same time, it is nice to be able to use one's expertise to help a friend, perhaps even to discover and encourage a good writer.

That said, Miss Manners will teach you how to get rid of all that unwanted material. It requires your learning a difficult English word: **No.**

"No, thank you, I have too much reading that I have to do, and it would be forever before I got to it."

"No, thank you, I make it a rule never to read friends' work—it's not fair to them, when I can't give it the attention it deserves." (A gentleman of Miss Manners' acquaintance promises, instead, "to give it the attention it deserves," but we will not deal in irony here.)

"No, I think it would be a mistake for me to look over your child's paper. As a teacher, I know that papers are used to diagnose the student's weaknesses, and having someone else work on the paper would only disguise them, so that your child would never learn to fix them. Besides, I'm an English professor. What if I worked on it and he still only got a B minus?"

DUCKING ADVICE

DEAR MISS MANNERS—Parent and child are shopping. Child wishes to buy expensive toy, which accompanying parent does not wish to purchase for him.

Casual acquaintance, a "nice" lady who simply adores children, sees the predicament and decides to settle the issue. She says, *"Oh, c'mon, buy it for him. He's your child! He won't be a child forever!"*

In this situation is it more proper for the parent to

1. Deliver swift kick to the shins of the nice lady, or
2. Tell her child, "Darling, did you hear that? This nice lady is going to buy it for you!"

What if it is candy, or something else that he is not supposed to have?

GENTLE READER—It is because she admires your refusal to allow your child to bludgeon you into buying things that Miss Manners is forced to point out that conning someone else into doing so, even as punishment for intrusiveness, is not the lesson you want to teach. Shin-kicking probably isn't either.

You may be sure, however, that Miss Manners supports you in rejecting attempts to undermine your authority. Whether it is presents or candy is irrelevant—the point is that the decisions are yours to make. What you might say is, **"You're exactly right, he is my child, and I have the responsibility of teaching him to grow up to be a considerate adult."** That a considerate adult does not interfere with child-rearing is left unspoken.

REFUSING FOOD

DEAR MISS MANNERS—Is there a gracious way to lose one's appetite? Sometimes, during an attack of nerves, I can't eat anything. This puts a crimp in dates and job interviews, which are the only situations when I get that nervous. It seems like bad strategy to let on about how anxious I am, but if I obeyed my companions' exhortations to "eat up," the result would be even more dramatically unpleasant. How can I refuse all or most of a meal without alarming potential suitors or employers?

GENTLE READER—There had better be a gracious way to avoid eating, because there is no gracious way to suffer the consequences at which you hint without casting aspersions on your dates and interviewers.

If it is of any comfort, Miss Manners will point out that the violation of etiquette is your companions'. It is polite to offer people food, but rude to monitor what they eat and attempt to force-feed them.

You must simply keep ignoring their exhortations, murmuring merely **"Thank you, it's delicious,"** without actually eating. Using the time that you would otherwise spend in chewing for charming conversation would be infinitely more to your advantage than using it to discuss your digestive system.

REFUSING DRINK

DEAR MISS MANNERS—I'm a young male in high favor of a reputable social life. Where I live, drinking is a big ingredient in nighttime social amusement.

Recently, I've decided to test myself by abstaining from any alcohol for some time. My friends and I still go out and have fun, but often I've run into confusion and odd responses by bartenders and other sociolites [*sic*].

My question is: What do you drink if you're not drinking? What beverages should you order in night spots, clubs and even formal dining situations? More importantly, how should I relate these sensible feelings to my friends without declaring the insensitive, "I'm on the wagon"?

GENTLE READER—When ordering a drink, either for oneself or through a host, it is customary to say what one wants, not what one doesn't want, nor why one doesn't want it.

Sociolites (Miss Manners adores the term; she knows exactly the sort of gregarious busybody you mean) should be discouraged from investigating the matter by a simple repetition of the order:

"I'll have a tomato juice, please." (The nonalcoholic drinks most readily available at bars are cocktail mixers: tonic water, club soda, juice or plain water.)

"What's the matter? Why aren't you drinking?"

"I am. I'd like a tomato juice, please."

"No, I mean why aren't you having a real drink?"

"I'd like a real tomato juice, please."

And so on, until you drive them to their own drinks and some other topic.

REFUSING TO DANCE

DEAR MISS MANNERS—Even though I can't dance to save my life, I do occasionally attend events or go to places where dancing is a prominently-featured activity. How do I gracefully decline an invitation to dance? And how do I respond to the not-infrequently-asked question, "Why aren't you dancing?"

GENTLE READER—What not to say, as Miss Manners is sure you have already discovered, is "I can't dance." That is a sure way to get dragged out onto the floor by someone who promises to teach you.

Even the more graceful "I prefer to watch you dance" may encourage an "Oh, come on" argument. The safest thing is not to answer the question, but to reverse the debate by saying **"Won't you join me in sitting one out?"**

REFUSING TO LEND

DEAR MISS MANNERS—I am a college student who thinks of books as precious possessions. Although it is a financial hardship at present to buy them, it is worth the expense because I often use the books for research ideas or as references.

I have cheerfully lent books to people over the years and, more often than not, they are not returned. Even if I could afford to replace them, many are out of print. I am no longer willing to lend books, cheerfully or otherwise. How does one politely turn down someone's request to borrow a book? I am desperate for your help; some of the "borrowers" are professors.

GENTLE READER—Book thievery is the one crime of which people do not seem to mind being suspected. If you said *"I never lend my tiara, because I might not get it back,"* it would be an insult. To say **"Oh, I'm so sorry, I just have a rule never to lend books—people fall in love with them and never return them"** is charming.

If the professor is your thesis adviser, you might volunteer to arrange to have the library send him or her its copy.

REFUSING TO GIVE TELEPHONE NUMBERS

DEAR MISS MANNERS—If you have an unlisted telephone number and don't want to give it out, how can you respond to somebody who asks for it, without giving offense?

GENTLE READER—By saying, politely, **"I'm so sorry, but it's impossible to reach me by phone—I don't even have an answering machine. But I'd love to hear from you"** (Miss Manners is assuming that the problem is with the telephone, not the individual applicant) **"and here's my address."**

This will undoubtedly cut down on the number of social advances you receive, but Miss Manners believes that people who do not respect other people's need for a peaceful home life would make bad friends anyway.

REFUSING SUPPLICATIONS

DEAR MISS MANNERS—One cannot walk the streets of any big city without passing a beggar who intones, "Can you spare some change?" or who simply rattles some coins in a plastic cup. I usually avert my eyes and try to ignore him, but that response denies the undeniable. The beggar is a person, and as such, he surely deserves, at a minimum, an acknowledgment of his existence.

In an effort to exhibit a semblance of humanity, I sometimes make eye contact and state simply, "Sorry, no." But that is not really acceptable, either. First, the answer is usually a lie, and second, the line is usually uttered with a measure of impatience or condescension that degrades us both. Is there any response that can uphold the dignity of both participants? Or is the encounter so inherently undignified that one should escape as quickly and quietly as possible?

GENTLE READER—Etiquette offers two rules about encounters with strangers in the street:

1. Observe the convention that they are invisible, because it is impossible to live in a city where you are constantly being required to participate in social encounters not of your own choosing.
2. Be kind to strangers in need.

The astute will observe that these are directly contradictory. This is not so much because Miss Manners and her ilk take amusement in causing confusion as because following rules of etiquette often requires making judgments based on the particular conditions.

Whether to acknowledge the approaches of beggars at all—like the question of whether to give them money—is a complicated issue, in which the possible good and the possible danger of the situation must be instantly assessed. But Miss Manners can deal definitively with your question of how to do it, if you so choose. So could you, if you were not being so literal-minded.

"Can you spare some change?" is an idiomatic expression meaning "Will you give me some change?" rather than an inquiry into the amount of your disposable income. Thus, **"Sorry, no,"** or better yet, the briefer **"Sorry,"** is a reasonable and polite answer.

CHAPTER 4

COMPLIMENTS

CONTEMPORARY VERSIONS

A selection of contemporary compliments:

"You look terrific—did you have a face-lift?"

"Wow, nice place. You must really be raking it in."

"So you finally took off all that weight. It certainly is an improvement."

"Great suit—how much did it run you?"

"You should dye your hair; people would take you for thirty."

"Another new outfit! You must be rolling in money."

"I see you had your teeth done—it's amazing what a difference it makes."

"Super earrings—are they real?"

"Your eyes are such a beautiful blue—contacts?"

"I love your apartment. Who'd you have do it?"

"You're really moving ahead. Your firm must have a real commitment to diversity."

"Is that all your own hair?"

Miss Manners has noticed that such compliments do not always produce the glow of happiness that was presumably intended. Some of those so honored will still smile and say **"Oh, thank you."** Then a vaguely troubled look sets in, as if they are puzzled about why they don't feel better after being complimented. Others just skip the possibility that a compliment was intended. They simply reply (warning to parents: The following language has been cleaned up—no,

mercilessly scrubbed free of all flavor—by Miss Manners):
"What's it to you?"

When the authors of these tributes notice that they are
not being credited with all the charm they intend, they get
snippy. Defendants in sexual harassment suits are not the
only people going around muttering "You can't even say
anything nice anymore."

Of course they blame Miss Manners. "You see?" they say
in bitter triumph, "there's no use trying to be polite. People
misinterpret it."

Not really. The problem is that they interpret it. Compliments are meant to be savored, so even the most ordinary
and offhanded ones are examined with great attention. In
their eagerness to believe anything favorable, people are apt
to overinterpret to the point of daftness:

"She said this was a nice shirt—do you think that means
she's in love with me?"

"He thought the client liked me. I don't think he'd say
that unless he was thinking of making me a vice president."

Yet even the vainest person would be taxed to find something flattering in the assumption that any improvement in
looks must have been accomplished by theatrical, if not sur-
gical, tricks—and was thought by everyone to be way over-
due. You are not going to know that those discerning people
have a few more suggestions for what should be done before
you finally pass muster. Nor is it heart-warming to feel that
people are assessing your possessions favorably while thinking that you are overspending for them or imagining how
much better your things would suit them than they do you.

Miss Manners is almost as dismayed as these poor souls
who had been momentarily deceived into thinking that others had admired their looks or their taste. Why, she asks

herself, is it now common to issue compliments that have a sting in them? Or rather (since it is not Miss Manners' job to police secret assumptions) why is this frankly stated to the person concerned?

Meanness, one might say. There are those who believe that the world has gotten so vicious that even niceness must be laced with little digs. Miss Manners tries not to succumb to such despair. Her slightly more charitable theory is that people think that compliments must be edged in order to be believable—that no one would believe in a kind thought, so it must be tempered with criticism or self-interest to be plausible.

The fact is that people do believe in compliments. That is why it is kind to offer them and unkind to modify them with additional comments that undo their effect.

GRUDGING COMPLIMENTS

DEAR MISS MANNERS—What is the best thing to do when someone you know has on a new outfit or is sporting a new hairdo that you don't particularly like, and she or he knows you notice? I don't want to lie and give an insincere compliment, but on the other hand, I want to acknowledge the new look in some way. Sometimes the change is too obvious not to notice.

I have the feeling that if I don't have anything positive to say, I should not say anything. I have been in this situation before, and I've just kept quiet. It's also happened to me recently. I was wearing my contact lenses instead of my glasses, and a new hairdo, and a coworker commented that I looked different. That was not a complimentary statement to me, especially the way she said it.

GENTLE READER—Let's see if Miss Manners understands all the options: You don't want to compliment someone if it doesn't strictly reflect your truthful opinion. But you feel you should say something. And you are on to those neutral comments that make it so glaringly obvious that they are substituting for compliments.

What is this? A multiple choice test in which all the answers have already been marked False? The only other possibility Miss Manners can imagine is a horrified "What have you done to yourself?"

She doesn't care for that. However, two out of your three rejected possibilities would pass the politeness test—silence and insincere compliments. What makes you think we are all obliged to notice one another's grooming habits? Or that saying something insincere just because it might please another person is a sin?

GRUDGING ACCEPTANCES

DEAR MISS MANNERS—My coworker commented on my haircut, saying, "Oh, look, Theresa cut her hair. It looks really nice."

I did not have a new style—my hair was just considerably shorter. As I was not comfortable with my new look, I found her comment unnerving and questioned her sincerity. Should one announce that another has cut her hair, or is it better to remain silent and pretend not to notice any difference? If one does comment, what is the most appropriate thing to say?

GENTLE READER—**"It looks really nice."**
Mind you, Miss Manners is not endorsing the idea of

announcing physical changes in other people. The workplace, especially, is plagued by those who go around monitoring personal appearances: *"Are you putting on weight?"* *"Another new outfit!"* *"Gee, you look terrible, what's the matter?"* *"You've dyed your hair!"* and so on.

Even compliments can be disastrous, as has to be explained to many a male worker who imagines the female workforce is delighted to be told how well it fills out its sweaters. Or to anyone who has assumed that weight loss is always a matter for congratulations, without considering that it can be a frightening symptom of serious disease.

So why is Miss Manners not taking up the cudgels on your behalf? Why isn't she quivering with indignation against your coworker, and alarm at your being unnerved?

Well, because it was such an offhand, innocuous, obviously well-meant comment. It may even have been prompted by the desire not to allow you to think that silence about the change meant your haircut was so awful that the less said about it the better.

It is wrong to scrutinize people for changes they might prefer to let pass, but Miss Manners is afraid it is even more wrong to examine their trivial remarks for lurking insults.

BEGRUDGING COMPLIMENTS

DEAR MISS MANNERS—My husband and I had our friends, a husband and wife, over for dinner one evening, and we were all talking and listening to music. She and I got up to go in the kitchen to get drinks, when my husband said to her husband, "Your wife is so pretty."

She and I both heard it loud and clear. She just giggled about it. I felt like someone had stabbed me in the heart, I was so hurt. I didn't feel it was proper to give a compliment of that nature to another man's wife, especially in front of me. It made me feel like an old dishrag. I told my husband how hurt I was, and that I thought it was wrong of him to say that, etc., etc. He says I am overreacting.

She and I have been very good friends for about six months, because we do the same kind of work and have children close in age. We talk to each other every day. Now I don't feel like socializing with them as couples. Once, my husband said how pretty her outfit was that she was wearing, and one time he said she has pretty eyes. These comments stung a little at the time, but I just forgot about them, but this recent comment really has bothered and hurt me deeply.

GENTLE READER—Miss Manners is afraid that if you believe that a loyal husband must not only believe his wife to be the prettiest woman in the world, but also the only pretty woman in the world, you are in for a lifetime of dishrag-hood—or deceit. Miss Manners hardly thinks that your husband is planning a campaign of seduction based on feeding the lady a line via her husband. The choice you now offer him is to defy you or to dissemble his feelings. Either way would give you a good chance to learn the meaning of that phrase about being stabbed in the heart, which you now use over a normal triviality.

Isn't your friend pretty? Then why not say so? In fact, you should be saying so. She is your friend, isn't she? Besides, agreeing with your husband's compliments is the most charming way to indicate your closeness in front of others.

OVERRESPONDING

DEAR MISS MANNERS—My hazel eyes turn a vivid, arresting shade of green when I wear my contact lenses, which is almost all the time. When people compliment me on "the greenest eyes since Vivien Leigh," I don't know what to say. It is not the same as receiving a compliment on a new dress or haircut. A "Thank you" seems so dishonest.

GENTLE READER—Miss Manners finds your idea of a compliment peculiar. As far as she knows, a compliment is merely a passing pleasantry, not the Congressional Medal of Honor of which you want to make sure you are worthy.

So please resist the temptation to argue back. Not only does this give a casual remark more importance than was intended, but it discourages nice people from saying nice things. You don't need to grow or otherwise produce everything yourself in order to receive praise for it. Selecting the dress is, for example, enough. You didn't have to weave the material, design the pattern and stay up all night stitching it.

Saying **"thank you"** is neither honest nor dishonest; it is polite. If you can manage to blush prettily at the same time, you need not confess that you got the blush from a compact.

RESPONDING MODESTLY

DEAR MISS MANNERS—My ten-year-old daughter looks just like me, and not a week goes by that someone doesn't mention the striking resemblance. I'm pleased that she's so obviously mine, but how do I respond without sounding conceited?

If I say "Thank you," I feel as though I'm implying that I'm so gorgeous, my daughter just received quite a compliment to look like me. Usually, I say something nebulous, such as "Do you really think so?" or "Lots of people say that."

A friend in the same situation says, "Yes, the poor thing!" The dear child looks crestfallen at this response.

GENTLE READER—Not only do you need a graceful routine to deal with this recurring remark, but so does your daughter. It is a service to children to work out with them a pleasant answer to perennial remarks to which there is no logical response, such as "My, you've grown" and "Where did you get your pretty hair?"

(The short answers to these are, respectively, **"Really?"** and **"Thank you,"** but the child who can come up with a joking reply that is not a put-down or otherwise rude is not to be discouraged.)

As you point out, you need one that allows you to be modest, without, as your friend is doing, extending your modesty to include your daughter. What is modesty to oneself can easily slip into insult when applied to another.

Fortunately, people are allowed some vanity on behalf of their relatives that they cannot display in connection with themselves. You can say: **"Well, I'm very flattered; I can't speak for Emily."** And then Emily should smile and, with the same license to take pride in family, say: **"I'm flattered, too."**

PATRONIZING COMPLIMENTS

Bicycling up the hill to get home, on the same route he has now taken for some 40 years, a gentleman of Miss Manners' acquaintance has begun to notice a change. He used to just peddle along without attracting any attention. Nowadays, young people along the street, or who speed past him on their bicycles, shout out "Right on!" or give him a thumbs up sign. He is neither encouraged, as is perhaps the intention of his cheering squad, nor charmed.

Miss Manners understands. Since her hair became a dainty white (it's not true that she took to powdering it, on the advice of her dear friend Madame de Staël), people have continually been announcing to her heartily, "I think it's great that you've let your hair turn." As if her hair had asked her permission to do so.

These reactions are not actually secret objections to growing older. Personally, Miss Manners had long been anticipating reaching what she considers to be a proper age. When she was a mere wisp of a thing, her dear father had said, "I can just picture you with a high-necked collar and a stick, tyrannizing over generations of the young," and ever since, she could hardly wait to grow into that vision.

There is just something unpleasantly patronizing about one person congratulating another for following the normal course of events. It is cheeky to assume that it took special effort to do so, and presumptuous to confer praise on that account.

People with disabilities loathe being told, as they constantly are, how courageous they are. They or anyone else may exhibit courage by electing to assume a burden that could be avoided. Not having chosen to undertake whatever difficulties they experience in their everyday lives, they are merely carrying on as best they can, and do not wish to be patted on the head for doing so.

Some people who are complimented for changing their appearances—who have, for example, lost weight or undergone cosmetic surgery—find themselves not so much thrilled at being complimented as they are dismayed at thus becoming retroactively aware how much improvement other people seem to have always thought they needed. (The reaction Miss Manners recommends is a nonspecific **"You look wonderful,"** uttered in a normal tone, as opposed to such amazed announcements as *"You finally did something about that nose of yours!"* and *"Wow, you must have taken off a ton!"*)

While Miss Manners realizes that few people nowadays are so fastidious as to be displeased with being complimented on the things they own—their clothes, their houses, their furniture—such remarks were long considered distasteful. Before the act of consumerism came to be thought of as the ultimate creative expression of the inner soul, there was an objection to having one's goods appraised, because the idea that you-are-what-you-buy is demeaning.

Why is Miss Manners being so churlish? Most people aren't offering misplaced compliments nowadays; they are freely insulting friend and stranger alike with taunts about one another's eating habits, taste in clothes, love lives and state of environmental awareness. Has Miss Manners lost her mind to start discouraging positive remarks? Is it even possible that there is such a thing as an impertinent compliment?

Well, yes. Miss Manners would not go so far as to allow anyone to take insult over an obviously well-meant comment. But those who offer such remarks should not be under the impression that they are conferring pleasure.

Praise is a wonderful thing, and we can all use more of it. However, the person who offers it must seem genuinely impressed, acknowledging the superiority of the object of praise. By condescending to validate something commonplace as if it were the best that could be expected, one puts oneself in the position of superiority.

Compliments that really mean "You're great for managing

to do what I take for granted," "It's amazing that you're not too discouraged to go on," "I see that you finally did something about the way you look," "I see that you decided not to do anything about the way you look" and "I approve of your personal choices" or "You're finally up to snuff" just do not manage to bring that flush of pleasure to the cheek.

CHAPTER 5

CONVERSATION

GAMBITS

"How's business?"

"Don't ask."

This is not the opening to a joke, you may be relieved to hear, but the opening to an etiquette directive, as you may be less relieved to hear.

A serious inquiry as to how business is going is appropriate when one is addressing one's employees or representatives of an enterprise in which one is thinking of investing. It is not appropriate for general conversation, especially among those who work in a world of downsizing, where it may provoke tears.

Actually, it has never been polite to inquire, under social conditions, about other people's professional success, much less to probe a possible lack of it. (It has never led to pleasant results.) Those who have wonderful things to report end up being accused of smugness, or, at best, being loved for something other than what they fondly think of as their true selves. Those with less end up feeling snubbed and unnecessarily apologetic.

American manners do not expressly prohibit discussing occupation-related topics, as do those of many countries, where even asking someone's occupation is considered tantamount to demanding to know how much money that person makes. Perhaps American leniency was a mistake. Miss Manners is considering revoking it altogether.

Many people really are offended when queried about their occupations. Some object because they feel that the inquirers will look down upon them when they receive the answer, and others because they feel the inquirers will look up to them for advice or assistance. The choice seems to be between "What do you think of me?" and "What do you want of me?"

In addition, no occupation is safe from its share of maddeningly predictable comments and jokes, along the lines of *"Oh, you're a zookeeper? Well, let me tell you, it's a zoo around here. And I suppose you're up to a lot of monkey business."* (Being terminally polite, Miss Manners always smiles pleasantly at people who remark, upon meeting her, *"Oh, I guess I'd better watch how I eat."* But after she's done smiling like that, she has to go and get her face defrosted.)

When you throw in the retired, parents-not-employed-outside-the-home, the unemployed and the undercover, Miss Manners is hard put to think of anyone at all who enjoys this sort of conversation. So Miss Manners is hereby declaring that a social **"What do you do?"** is only proper if it is immediately followed by **"I thought so—I've been searching high and low for someone of your skills. Is there any chance you would give me a call tomorrow at my office?"**

Worse still, a show of interest in another's work too often slips over to a show of interest in the financial yield. From the attempt to make the question seem a matter of general interest *("Has the economy affected you much?")* to the bald inquiry (all authors are routinely asked *"How is your book selling?"*) these questions translate smack into "How much money do you make?"

Miss Manners suspects that things may have deteriorated

to the point where she cannot assume that it is obvious why it is impolite to inquire into the finances of others. She can just hear the same people who go around asking others when they are planning to get married or have children, whether they considered or had plastic surgery, whether or not they have found God and what is their age, weight, sexual orientation and brand of automobile, justify their nosiness with a proud declaration of interest in humanity and curiosity about individuals.

Miss Manners could tell them exactly why it is rude to ask nosy questions, but she has decided to let them wonder. **She doesn't care to say.** That, in case anyone needs to know, is the polite way of saying *"None of your business."*

Then one is obliged to get the socializing back on track by starting over, foraging for a topic of mutual interest. This is done by putting forth a collection of bland observations until one of them is seized upon and developed. So one might just as well start out that way.

OCCUPATIONAL HAZARDS

DEAR MISS MANNERS—When I meet someone new and the fact that I am a college mathematics instructor comes up, I almost always get one of two responses.

The first is *"Math is/was my worst subject,"* or *"I don't understand math at all."*

I acknowledge that math is considered difficult by many people, but I try to remain positive about things. So I reply that some things in life can be hard to understand at first, but with a lot of work and patience, one can achieve success in almost anything, including math. But they usually just ignore this reply and insist, sometimes angrily, that math is just too challenging for them. I am at a loss as to how to continue the conversation from there.

The second, more callous, response is, *"I hate math"* or *"I don't see how anyone could like math."* Someone asked, *"You mean you like math enough to teach it??"* while contorting her face as if I had just told her I enjoy eating worms.

I calmly replied that I did, indeed, like math that much. If I were introduced to a country music singer, it would be considered inappropriate to say, "You mean you like country music enough to sing it??" So why is it accepted, perhaps even fashionable, to make similar remarks about math?

With either response, I immediately feel put on the defensive about my field. I do not feel obligated to apologize for my interest in math, nor do I feel responsible for the lack of success in math of people I have never even met before. But it's come to the point where I sometimes dread being asked what I do for a living, knowing the type of conversation that will ensue. How do I respond politely to these remarks?

GENTLE READER—If it is any comfort to you, there isn't an occupation in the world that doesn't call forth some obvious and generally not-very-kind remark. That attacking people to their faces is extremely rude is apparently not recognized, because, as you have seen, people do it all the time. If it's not over a job, it's over health, eating habits, weight, clothes, nationality, even neighborhood.

So you might practice a weak smile or the statement **"Oh, really."** Notice that there is no question mark at the end, nor should you produce an interrogative expression. You surely don't want to encourage these people to dig more deeply into their opinions.

AVOIDING THE HAZARD

DEAR MISS MANNERS—I work on stage and in the motion picture business in a technical position. Invariably, someone I meet socially will hear about this and ask, *"How do they do such-and-such?"* or, even worse, *"Oh, have you worked with any famous people? What are they like?"*

I'm proud of the work and enjoy my job, but I'd rather not give out my resume at social gatherings. How does one cut off people seeking professional advice in social settings?

GENTLE READER—If people were stopping you at parties to say *"I've always felt I would make a terrific movie star; can you put in a good word for me?"* or asking you for help with their home movies, you could say **"Oh, I come to parties to escape work."**

But what you describe—overinterest in one's profession, prompting questions one has heard too often already—is, while a nuisance, not the serious etiquette transgression of requesting professional advice when out socially. One discourages further questions by answering in a boring manner (**"Oh, I forget," "You know, I never could tell one actor from another"**) and then proposing other topics for discussion.

PRESUMPTION OF INNOCENCE

DEAR MISS MANNERS—George and I come from different social backgrounds. His family and most of his friends are of upper class status, and I was raised in a middle class, honest, hard-working family with many siblings. He is a fine, loving man whose manners are impeccable, but I find that some of his friends need improvement.

Occasionally when I am introduced to a "friend" for the first time, he will ask, "Who were you?"

I feel like replying, "I am the same person I've always been. Why? Is one expected to be SOMEBODY?"

I have not discussed this with George, but I believe he senses my discomfort. In most cases, he steps in and changes the subject. I know he is proud of me and affectionate and attentive. I was not from the wrong side of the tracks. In this day and time, it appalls me when people treat others like a gold-digger or the maid who married the master.

No, I do not have an inferiority complex. I am proud of whence I came and of my life. The geography of my past has never been an issue to my husband, nor my lack of prominence. We live in the south, where hospitality and congeniality flourish, but these jocks are real jerks.

GENTLE READER—The list of innocent questions that strangers who meet socially can use to get to know one another is getting shorter every day. *"What do you do?"* has come to be interpreted to mean "Are you important enough for me to spend time with you?" *"Where are you from?"* is taken as a demographic slur.

You are taking an inquiry about your family to mean a social slur (which, by the way, is how Miss Manners would classify your uncharming phrase "the wrong side of the tracks").

Miss Manners would like to see the presumption reinstated that people do not go around offering insults as social openers. Generally, they are just trying to establish, purely for the sake of getting into conversation, whether they know people in common or share interests.

This does not mean you need answer any of these questions directly. All that is required is to help start a conversation. Thus, the question about your background could be answered humorously, or even ignored, as long as you show a friendly demeanor by continuing, for example by asking your interlocutor—oh, something that cannot be taken as an insult.

FURTHER PRESUMPTION OF INNOCENCE

DEAR MISS MANNERS—Organized sports such as football and baseball hold no interest for me, and I do not watch them on TV or follow sports on the radio or in the newspapers. I have no idea, nor do I care, who is playing or which team has won or lost.

I am sick and tired of people putting me on the spot and implying that my indifference toward these activities is abnormal. Just yesterday, someone said (in an incredulous, "you're weird" tone of voice), "You mean to say you have no emotion or excitement at all about who wins the Super Bowl??!"

Can you please help me come up with a response that will make them realize I have the right to be uninterested in something that they may be passionate about and that it is rude to imply that I am deficient if I don't feel the same way?

GENTLE READER—Now, now. Miss Manners realizes any remark nowadays is an opportunity to bristle about rights and slurs. But you do not seem to recognize an idle conversation opener when you hear one.

"How 'bout them [name of home team]?" and "Who're you rooting for?" are about as challenging questions as "Cold [or hot] enough for you?" or "Think we're going to get some rain?" Replying by announcing that you have no interest in sports is as prissy and off-putting as rejecting a discussion of the weather with the statement that you do not follow meteorology. All you really need to do is to make some sociable sound to indicate that you accept the goodwill intended. **"Gee, I don't know; who do you think is going to win?"** is a good one, but even **"Haven't been following it lately"** will do if said pleasantly.

THE WEATHER

No general topic of conversation has as bad a reputation as the weather. Talking about the weather is considered by all to be the classic sign of social desperation.

But if there is one thing Miss Manners has learned from observing social life, it is that bad reputations seldom discourage popularity. Indeed, weather talk retains its popularity even though those who engage in it all harbor the sheepish feeling that they should say something more original.

No, they shouldn't. Please not. Miss Manners deeply believes that everyone should keep saying **"Hot enough for you?" "Looks like rain," "Winters just aren't the same as when I was young"** and **"You could fry an egg on the sidewalk today."**

Mind you, she is not requesting a tremendous amount of elaboration on these thoughts. The bodily changes that have led the speaker to expect rain need not be described, and we can probably do without extrapolations about the degenerative effects of mild weather on the already deplorably feeble character of the young.

But those basic weather remarks are nice and comforting and time-tested, and they do not scare off new acquaintances or old friends. This is a lot more than can be said for what passes for conversational originality. Sometimes Miss

Manners fears that people draw their favorite topics for general conversation from a list of what doctors, lawyers and members of the clergy are legally protected from divulging about their clients.

Why do they think we go to all that trouble to have weather? There is nothing like it when strangers are searching for a topic that will allow them to learn something about each other, or when acquaintances want to reaffirm their goodwill without taking the time for a discussion.

Under such conditions, the weather shines. There isn't anybody who can't contribute to the subject. No one takes offense, because it is no disgrace—rather a matter of pride—to live in a place with a dreadful climate. It can provide a complete and satisfying exchange, or it can be used to lead a conversation on to just about any other topic.

Let us say you find yourself in the grocery line behind someone you know but can't quite place, or you open the door to the person who periodically sprays your apartment to discourage minor wildlife. If you said, *"I see you're buying a lot of potato chips,"* or *"You look great in that uniform,"* you risk some funny looks. An exchange of views might slow down your day or theirs. But when one of you says **"Kind of muggy out today"** and the other replies **"Sure is,"** a pleasant and safe little affirmation of human benevolence has taken place.

For people who have just met, the weather is even more useful. One person says something like, **"We seem to have been having an unusual number of thunderstorms lately."** The reply indicates where the second person wants to take the conversation—**"Really? I've been studying so hard I didn't notice"** or **"I hate it because it's kept me from bicycling"** or **"Yes, and it's so poetic"**—and the next thing you know, the two of them are off having a cozy drink.

It is when an effort is made to avoid mentioning the weather that things get rough. As there isn't much to go on when meeting a stranger, all the originals seize upon one of the same four clues. Talk about social desperation.

Inevitably they ask questions or, worse, hazard guesses or, even worse, make jokes, based on the person's name, occupation, place of residence or origin or looks. But the stranger has had that name, occupation and so on for a long time and has heard all possible remarks they can inspire—and a few they shouldn't. Having hated the standard joke on one's name since kindergarten, taken regular offense at remarks about one's accent, gone to great lengths to avoid being asked the same ignorant questions about one's profession and endured the humiliation of having one's height, weight or hair color become a subject of wonder, one is rarely charmed by being told the obvious.

In comparison, a remark such as **"I don't mind the heat so much, but I can't stand the humidity"** (or its newer opposite number, **"I can take the cold, but what really gets me is the windchill factor"**) seems positively refreshing.

BANNED TOPICS

Here is a list of topics that polite people do not bring into a social conversation:

Sex; religion; politics; money; illness; the food before them at the moment and which foods they customarily eat or reject and why; anything else having to do with bodily functions; occupations, including their own and inquiries into anyone else's; the looks of anyone present—especially to note any changes, even improvements, since these people were last seen; and the possessions of anyone present, including their hosts' house and its contents and the clothing being worn by them and their guests, even favorably.

Those are only the traditionally banned topics. Miss Manners has been steadily adding to the list of what is likely to be explosive or soporific.

It is barely possible that the reasons for your divorce aren't covered under sex or money—nevertheless, the whole topic is socially banned. Perhaps neither religion nor politics adequately describes your feelings about how terribly people are treating animals, vegetables or minerals—also banned. So are descriptions of computer software and hardware, and recitals of the plots of movies or books.

Do you begin to see why the world needs misbehaving athletes? Or, as everyone can be loudly heard to be thinking, fewer etiquette rules?

However, those who believe that all topics should be permitted would do well to remember when the airing of bigotry and sexism, whether in the form of jokes or observations, went unchallenged by social disapproval. Or they might remember longingly the time when obscene language and vulgarity were muted by social disapproval.

Miss Manners recognizes that the relaxation of the old rules has permitted a few gratifying compliments—along with a lot of embarrassing personal remarks and intrusions. She understands that people's work and interests may coincide to produce interesting conversation about their fields— and a great risk of boring shop talk and vulgar networking.

Among sensible people, how much they spend is considered to be not unrelated to how much they have. This is why prices, like salaries, are not discussed in polite society. However, you will be glad to hear that acknowledged bargain hunters, who regard shopping as a sport, are allowed to compare their triumphs among themselves.

But she balks at the idea that we can all now be trusted to

enliven our social lives by discussing important political, social and religious issues. How enlightening or enjoyable is social conversation among an assortment of people who have strong feelings about, say, the morality of abortion, assisted suicide or capital punishment, the effects on society of the welfare system or affirmative action, or whether sex education or prayer should be permitted in public schools?

It isn't as though etiquette is opposed to airing controversy. On the contrary (so to speak): It prides itself on its specialty of providing rules for the very situations where controversial matters are most strenuously contested, such as courtrooms, classrooms or meetings. Etiquette (usually supplied by the rules of order of Miss Manners' colleagues Messrs. Robert or Riddick) is what keeps debate fair and to the point, rather than allowing one person to dominate or the whole thing to deteriorate into an exchange of insults.

But such rules cannot be invoked in social settings. Lightly held views and topics of no tremendous weight to those present may be bandied about pleasantly. People who trust one another enough to be able to discuss one of the supercharged topics peacefully (possibly because they are superpolite in spite of their differences, but more likely because they are all on the same side) may also do so without interference from etiquette, which knows enough not to disturb people who are having a good time.

However, confirmations of opinions already held and exercises in faking respect for people whose stupid or vicious opinions differ from one's own should not be confused with meaningful exchanges. So it isn't Miss Manners who is banning the casual airing of important topics; it is human nature.

SMALL TALK

DEAR MISS MANNERS—I used to have a job where I worked outside in both cold and hot weather, and I am now a messenger, who must go outside a few times a day for a short while. At both jobs, people say, "It's so hot, how can you stand it?" or, when it's raining, "I don't envy you having to go out in this weather." Or they say my job must be boring, or "You must hate it."

These people are strangers. I would sometimes reply, *"Are you going to give me some money so I don't have to?"* or *"Do you work in the White House?"* (meaning to be sarcastic, as in "I guess you have a great job"). I feel that commenting on the unfortunateness of someone's situation when a person has not complained or cannot change it is wrong. Please tell me the correct way to respond.

GENTLE READER—All right, but first Miss Manners insists that you have to understand to what you are responding.

The statements you report are not pitying or scornful commentaries on a difficult and perhaps unrewarding form of employment that you are forced to undertake for your daily sustenance, and which your interlocutors are expressing thanks to escape.

They are, rather, intended to convey a general sense of amiability and common humanity, in which the tone, rather than the choice of words, contains the substance of the message. In other words, these people are making small talk. Lighten up.

As a matter of fact, most of them are probably thinking what a free and glamorous life you lead, compared to most of the population, cooped up during working hours within sight of a supervisor. Your response is all right if you want to turn this into an embarrassed and fleeting sense that you really are to be pitied. If it were Miss Manners, she would prefer to say **"No, I love the outdoor life. Healthiest job in the world."**

BLATHER

DEAR MISS MANNERS—How is one to handle those people who, under the mask of a smile or other cordiality, throw verbal hand grenades into a conversation?

A relative who had invited us for the weekend greeted us—at the door!—with, *"I feel awful; I wish I'd told you not to come."* We had driven 100 miles, and we do, by the way, have a phone.

A client of mine greeted me at her granddaughter's wedding reception by saying, *"I never see you without thinking of all that money we lost on the investment you recommended."*

As openers, these leave me speechless, but they come from the person, more than the situation, and, as such, are not, unfortunately, onetime occurrences. If Miss Manners could offer some suggestions as to how I might, with exquisite politesse, lay them out, I would be eternally grateful.

GENTLE READER—These dreadful remarks are not, as Miss Manners is sure you realize, calculated insults. They are what she calls Blather—stupid, hurtful things that people say because they haven't done any thinking first.

The cure is to make them realize what they have said by replying to it seriously, which will then force them to retract it. The relative with the appalling greeting should be told, **"Oh, how awful that we've come at a bad time. We'll turn** right around. **Could we just come in for a minute, please, because we've been on the road for several hours, but then we'll be out of your way."**

The equally rude grandmother should be told, **"I'm terribly sorry that didn't work out better, but I don't want to spoil this occasion for you. Let me just give my best wishes to everyone and then I'll leave so I don't upset you."**

"HOW DOES THAT MAKE YOU FEEL?"

So. How do you feel about . . . How do you feel about being constantly asked how you feel?

This inquiry has replaced condolences. If something awful happens to you, the response is less likely to be an expression of shock than a maddeningly superior *"Would you like to talk about how this makes you feel?"*

It has replaced congratulations. If something wonderful happens, you are less likely to have your delight echoed by others than to have them inquire solemnly as to the exact state of your feelings—as if, deep down, you should be worrying about the possible adverse side effects of your luck, rather than exulting in it.

It has replaced ordinary conversation with a kind of dour and pessimistic mutual temperature-taking. Lest anyone should treat lightly an inquiry into his or her feelings, a positive response, however true, may be supplemented with the dire *"Yes, but how do you really feel?"*

Also, there is no answer. It's as if the uncle who annually used to boom out in front of everyone on your birthday "Tell us how it feels to be—" (whatever age you had just turned) has taken over society.

How does Miss Manners feel about this? She feels strange

about being so annoyed at this ubiquitous question, which has raced along that well-traveled road from psychotherapy to television babble to daily conversation.

It is, after all, one of the missions of her life to impress upon a me-first world that the feelings of others should be of paramount consideration in determining one's own behavior. Is it not, therefore, progress that so many people are taking the trouble to find out what the feelings of their fellow creatures are?

Miss Manners is also one of the great defenders (perhaps the only one left) of expressions of conventional pleasantry, which aren't supposed to mean anything other than a pledge of goodwill. Yet Miss Manners refuses to admit "How do you feel?" to this category until certain conditions have been met.

1. People who ask this question must stop acting as if they are conferring some tremendous act of charity on the afflicted. If it is to be no more than a conventional expression, there is no cause for smug self-congratulation. They get credit for politeness, but not great humanitarianism.

2. There must be a conventional answer available to those who do not wish to respond to a request to discuss their feelings, and it must be graciously accepted. Under normal circumstances, **"Fine, thank you, how do you feel?"** should do. For tragic circumstances, **"Thank you, I'll be all right"** should evoke **"Please let me know if there's anything I can do,"** rather than pressure along the lines of *"But you'll feel better if you talk about it."*

Mind you, Miss Manners agrees that the world would be a better place if we learned to fathom other people's feelings. She is sorry to have to point out that the best way of doing this is not always the direct way of asking. Many events do not produce feelings that lend themselves to being articulated. What did you reply when your uncle asked you how it felt to be eleven?

There are also times when one simply does not want to expose one's feelings to anyone who happens to ask. Confiding deep feelings is a privilege of intimate friendship, not to be promiscuously bestowed, whatever you have observed on daytime television. Those who are willing to serve others in the valuable office of confidant and sounding board need to offer a history of sympathetic, but nonintrusive interest and the demonstrable ability to keep a secret. This cannot be achieved merely by setting up an inquiry.

There is no substitute, Miss Manners is afraid to say, for learning to observe the feelings of others from their behavior, and for using the imagination and one's own feelings to guess at common humanity. Demanding to be told can be a rude substitute for these civilized skills.

So. How does that make you feel?

CHANGING THE SUBJECT

DEAR MISS MANNERS—The only topic of conversation that my elderly parents and relatives really enjoy discussing any more is their medical problems—not just a summary, but all of the intimate details (e.g., toilet problems, ear cleaning, polyp removal), which can be disgusting at times, particularly at the dinner table. I am sympathetic to these concerns, but if I try to change the subject to a non-medical topic, my parents and relatives become visibly annoyed with me.

They have had their share of problems, but are not hospitalized. They still want to live on their own and are healthy enough to do it. I understand that medical problems are scary and that talking about them can reduce the anxiety, but do we have to get into detail, particularly at the dinner table? A summary should be sufficient, with reasonable time permitted for discussion of other topics of common interest. What do you suggest?

GENTLE READER—That you come up with some topics of equal interest. Miss Manners warns you that it isn't going to be easy to compete with the fascination of documenting one's own deterioration. But since you can't bark at your elders "that's not dinner table conversation!" the way they used to at you, and since you don't want to seem unsympathetic, this is your only hope.

The unfortunate preoccupation you describe is, in people who are not actively suffering from medical problems, a sign of slackening interest in the future. While everybody else is curious about what is happening in the world and anxious about his or her own progress, they feel they have no stake in it.

By bringing up events in the news so as to suggest that you would like opinions on it from their accumulated wisdom, and by mentioning events in your own life as if you were interested in receiving their guidance (the latter to be done carefully, with an unspoken lack of commitment to abide by advice and an avoidance of topics on which you are sensitive) you may be able to turn their attention outwards. Miss Manners wishes you luck for their sake, even more than for yours.

"ARE YOU MARRIED?"

DEAR MISS MANNERS—Say we have just been introduced at a social function, and are making the usual small talk. With no hint of motive, you ask if I am married. In the same conversation tone, and without attempting to sound coy, I respond, "No, not legally," or "Technically, no." What would your reaction be?

The reality is that I am a gay man involved in a long standing, committed relationship. Marital status being the subject of state law, my lover and I cannot be "married." But your question does not seek to know how I am regarded by the government and the IRS; you want to know how I am integrated in the social fabric.

If I respond simply "no" or "yes," I allow you to proceed with a misunderstanding that could eventually cause you embarrassment. If I divert our conversation to explain the circumstances, I run the risk of sounding militant or of making this aspect of my life seem overriding. I do not want to create the impression that my homosexuality defines my work as a lawyer, board member or responsible citizen, but I will not be a dissembler, either.

My usual response always raises eyebrows, but it allows the other person to determine whether a more detailed explanation will be pursued. In terms of keeping the conversational door open, it has met with varying degrees of success. Does Miss Manners regard this as unduly provocative, and if so, can she suggest a more appropriate tack?

GENTLE READER—On the contrary, she would like to thank you for this solution, which meets her criteria on two major counts: It answers the question that was really being asked, rather than the literal one, and it deals with the social, rather than the private, nature of your personal life.

When Miss Manners has attempted to explain the latter, she has been attacked from two sides, on the equally erroneous assumptions that she is either promoting or suggesting hiding nonlegal partnerships, whatever the gender component.

Miss Manners doesn't endorse anyone's personal arrangements, not even their legal marriages. It is not her business to do so. What she asks is a single standard for everyone, of telling society simply what it needs to know—as you put it "how I am integrated in the social fabric," or, more plainly, whether you are unattached, and if not, whom should I invite when I invite you.

"DO YOU HAVE CHILDREN?"

DEAR MISS MANNERS—Because my husband is a minister, I frequently find myself in small talk with people I don't know well: parishioners, their visiting friends and relations, other clergy, persons attending judicatory events, etc. Often people ask me, "Do you have children?"

Although this is a painful question for me, since my husband and I are in the midst of sorting out and treating multiple fertility problems, I realize that most people are asking quite innocently, in an attempt to open avenues of possible conversation. Usually I answer, "No, I do not." Sometimes, it is appropriate for me to add, "Do you?" which launches the conversation in a different direction, but often that is not a sensible reply.

I expect people simply to let the matter drop when I tell them I have no children. Instead, I have been the recipient of the most appalling remarks, including:

"Isn't it wonderful that young people can choose not to have children these days without society being critical of their choices?"

"You ought not to wait too long, you know, or you could have medical difficulties."

"You're such a feminist, you probably couldn't handle the demands of children."

"You really ought to see a doctor. They can do a lot these days for people without children."

"Oh, do you have some kind of problem?"

Sometimes I make a vague response, such as "Well, we haven't had such good luck so far," but this rarely stops the determined, who continue with their line of questioning. Often I wind up feeling just dreadful, fighting back tears, and making graceless efforts to change the topic. I prefer not to offend these clods, because of my husband's position. Any suggestions on how to handle the situation?

GENTLE READER—Miss Manners keeps trying to handle it from the other end, but, as you have noticed, determinedly intrusive people are not easily squelched.

They can, however, be distracted. It is a great deal of fun to hand out advice, as no one knows better than Miss Manners, but oddly enough, most people consider it even more fun to talk about themselves. The solution to your problem is a quick attack of counterquestioning. Miss Manners trusts that you will limit it to reasonably impersonal questions— "Do you live near here?" "Have you visited here before?" and so on. The idea, as you point out, is to find a topic of conversation.

For this purpose, "Do you have children?" is not offensive, provided it is dropped after a negative answer. Miss Manners doesn't see why it isn't sensible for you to return it with everyone except the never-married—it is not an inappropriate question for the elderly, for example. Of course one can hardly ask it of children, but Miss Manners doubts they are the ones giving you gynecological advice.

ENDING DISCUSSION

Dear Miss Manners—I was wearing some particularly expensive cologne, and a friend who is not very well-to-do complimented me on it and asked its name. When I replied, she remarked, *"Oh, that's expensive!"*

I was tempted to reply, "Oh, it's not that expensive," in order to not make her feel bad that she couldn't afford it, but then I realized that it would sound like money meant nothing to me. So I foolishly replied, "Yes, it is," and then wanted to bite my tongue. How would you have handled the situation?

Gentle Reader—By asking, **"Is it."**

Miss Manners has omitted the question mark here, because the voice should not rise interrogatively. Properly pronounced, it should have the same effect as politely saying "I don't find this a proper subject for discussion."

For dogged questioners, it also has the advantage of suggesting that no lady needs to interest herself in the price of perfume because (1) she always receives it as a present or (2) she got it at a discount. Which this is, Miss Manners would not dream of saying.

CONFESSION AS CONVERSATION

Miss Manners has noticed that offering oneself as an example has become a social form. Privately and publicly, more and more people are moved to tell their personal experiences to others. There is no stage of life for which countless case histories are not constantly made available by their subjects, and there is no anxiety, tragedy, illness or vice that has not organized its "support system" of similarly afflicted people. What used to be considered highly confidential information is routinely pooled among acquaintances and strangers alike.

Miss Manners is sensible to the benefits of sharing information, exchanging advice and receiving reassurance and encouragement from people in a similar state as oneself. Feeling that one is not alone in one's troubles has always been a comfort.

But as personal confession has become standard behavior, it has taken on unpleasant characteristics associated with that which is proclaimed to be "normal." Soon we shall require a support group to help people who have become the victims of any of the following delusions.

1. *That everything hidden is shameful.*

There is such a thing as privacy, after all. Not everyone wants to hear the details of everyone else's lives, nor to make his or her own troubles into community property. People who do not care to share are often bullied now, as if failure to tell all indicates that one is ashamed.

2. *That everyone who is told what used to be called secrets is bound by the standards associated with the medical and legal professions.*

People who unburden themselves freely cannot then become indignant when others allow this information to pass into their own conversation. With each passing, the obligations become weaker. At the very least, one should assume that one's confidants indulge in pillow talk, and these days it is hard to know how many pillows may be involved.

3. *That what works for one person ought to work for another.*

Aside from the fact that it is not really helpful to advise unattached people to get married, there is a real danger in attempting to establish patterns of living as normal, even ones that are statistically prevalent. Ladies, in particular, are always being subjected to one-size-fits-all advice. Wouldn't you think that people who had been subjected to one-size-fits-all pantyhose would know better?

UNWANTED CONFIDENCES

DEAR MISS MANNERS—What is the appropriate response when someone in a conversation, either professional or personal, begins to tell you all about their personal problems that are bothering them—and then, after delivering the unwanted and unsolicited gripe session, they say, "I know you don't want to hear all this, do you?"

Should one be polite but dishonest (and at the same time invite further unwanted conversation) by saying, "Oh, sure, I'm enjoying this"? Or would an honest but rude affirmative response be appropriate? I am, of course, ruling out a sarcastic answer, such as "Sure, I haven't had my daily quota of vile and hateful conversation yet."

GENTLE READER—Miss Manners just hates that choice between rudeness and dishonesty. People keep setting it up for her, and she refuses to choose. She wants both—oops, she means neither.

One cannot admit to being bored by other people's confidences, however dreary. The honesty of it does not cancel out the cruelty. But one should not have to listen to all that either. A preferable way to stop it is by protesting, as if regretfully, **"It's just that I'd prefer you didn't tell me anything you want kept confidential."**

The witless will be disabused of the illusion that others will be more discreet about them than they are themselves.

Even the most dedicated blabbermouth will be reluctant to lose control of the story.

GOSSIP

It is just as well that we no longer consider gossiping a criminal offense, as was the case some centuries ago. The jails are overcrowded as it is. We would have to put bars around the whole population.

Nor does Miss Manners care for the current approach by which passing around gossip is treated as a virtue and gossips are congratulated for repeating comments that do serious damage. Here's the way it works:

The gossip corners the target and says something like, *"I think you should know what people are saying about you,"* or (specifically quoting one person) *"I know he's a friend of yours so he probably hasn't talked to you about this, but I think you ought to know how he really feels."*

What follows is some awful criticism—*"Everybody thinks you've gotten full of yourself"* or *"He doesn't want to hurt you, but he told me that he thinks you're behaving like a fool"*—which naturally makes the target cringe.

Noticing this reaction—who can help noticing the way people reel when they receive a severe psychological blow?—the gossip switches tones: *"Oh, I shouldn't have told you. I feel terrible. I didn't know you'd take it this way. I just thought you'd want to know. I should have kept my mouth shut."*

This is no more than the simple truth, except for the part about not knowing how the person would take it. How does anyone expect people to take being told nasty opinions of themselves, especially when these are accompanied by the information that such unpleasantries are in general circulation? Where did we get the idea that people are supposed to be able to accept this kind of thing without flinching?

Yet that is what everyone tries valiantly to do. Pitifully, the victims try to arrange their faces in an interested smile, and then they reply, "No, no, please, you did the right thing to tell me. What else did they say?"

"I'm not going to tell you. I can see it's upset you, so just forget it. Pretend I never said anything."

Forget it? Forget that the pleasant lull that enables us all to face the mirror long enough to brush our teeth—the delusion that everyone who is not a known enemy thinks and speaks kindly of us—has been shattered? Forget the dizzying feeling that trusted people have been secretly engaged in sabotage?

"Oh, please tell me. It doesn't bother me. Honestly. I appreciate your telling me. It's good to bring these things out in the open. It clears the air. My feelings aren't hurt. I think it's good to know what people really think. I'm glad you told me." And so on, depending on how long it takes to flatter the gossip into continuing the torture. Having suffered the initial humiliation, the poor victim is reduced to begging for more.

As distasteful as Miss Manners finds this all-too-common scene, she does not blame it on the very human habit of gossiping. We are all, after all, observers of the human scene. Most gossip drifts idly along, interesting and amusing people without being taken very seriously. Sophisticated people know that the habit of passing on titillating information without having subjected it to rigorous investigation, or any investigation at all, is practically universal. And that mildly critical comments that the critic doesn't mean or doesn't consider important are often made for the sake of illustrating a point in the conversation, getting off a good crack, or ventilating some momentary pique. People do not always say unreservedly complimentary things about those whom they really do admire.

That is, everybody realizes this when gossiping or hearing gossip about others. The same sort of thing said about oneself seems proof of deep animosity, cunningly concealed, perhaps for years, by the pretense of fondness. The idle comment, idly—or perhaps not so idly—repeated, assumes frightening importance. Relationships are fractured. So is the perhaps unrealistic, but nevertheless essential, idea that one's charms outshine one's faults.

Miss Manners is tired of hearing people being thanked for stirring up this kind of trouble. She strongly advises victims of this practice to learn to direct their indignation where it really belongs. Rather than *"Oh, tell me more,"* it would be useful to learn to ask, **"Does he know you're telling me this? Because we are great friends, and I certainly wouldn't want him to think we've been maligning him behind his back."**

RELIGION

DEAR MISS MANNERS—I take my young son to church a few times each year so that he can make up his own mind, but I have no interest in religion myself.

For some unknown reason, my dentist told my real estate

agent that I'm a very religious person. So now, in an effort to please her client, the agent brings religion into our business discussions—"Sunday is the Lord's day, so let's have your open house on Saturday." To make matters worse, my real estate agent then told my tax accountant, so now, in an effort to please his client, he brings religion into our business discussions—"What does God want you to do in this case?"

All of this piety is driving me crazy. Short of moving to another town, how can I stop it?

GENTLE READER—With a modest principle of manners that fits right in with the moral principle you advocate.

You believe that one should be allowed to make up one's own mind about religion. Miss Manners believes that one should be allowed to make up one's own mind about whether one wishes to discuss one's religion or, as the case may be, its absence.

Although these people are not exactly proposing a theological discussion, you may treat their remarks as such and reply firmly, **"I don't discuss religion."** No doubt some will think it's further evidence of your extreme piety, but at least they will no longer trouble you.

DISHONESTY

DEAR MISS MANNERS—Occasionally someone says or does something that I really disapprove of. I don't want to lecture that person, obviously; yet I do not like to let the person think that I approve of their behavior.

My hostess said she hoped I liked the picnic table we were eating off, because her husband made it from lumber he had stolen. At a luncheon, one of the ladies (?) asked to take the receipt home to add to her husband's receipts that he saves for tax purposes. We had all paid for our meals and it was a large sum. Of course, others went on to say that was great as they always put their intimate dinners with their husbands on his expense account.

Is there a perfect response?

GENTLE READER—**"You're joking, of course. We all know you're an honorable person."**

Please do not mess with this perfect response by pointing out to Miss Manners that it is not literally accurate. Honor in etiquette sometimes demands setting standards higher than those in practice and encouraging people to live up to them.

MODESTY

DEAR MISS MANNERS—When I decided to attend graduate school, I applied to several, hoping that at least one would find me competent. Much to my surprise, a university in the northeast with a good reputation and name-recognition has invited me to attend.

Of course I am elated, and I shared the news with a few close friends. Word quickly spread, and I have heard comments ranging from sincere congratulations to the *"Gee, I didn't know you were that smart"* and *"What did you do to get in there?"*

I have thanked well-wishers who offered congratulations; however, I have either chuckled or simply not responded to the other comments, not knowing what to say. Were these people rude, or am I over-reacting?

GENTLE READER—No, you're doing fine. Just keep chuckling hollowly and referring to your school as A University in the Northeast. People will go on making those remarks, which are silly but not meant to be rude. They have been successfully annoying your school fellows this way for 360 years now, so why should they stop?

You are only allowed to retaliate by refusing to pronounce the name of the school, a tradition with which your school fellows will be familiar. Miss Manners offers you a sterling example in the following exchange that was reported to her by a lady of her acquaintance.

First Mother: Where's your son going to college?
Second Mother: In the Northeast.
First Mother: Really? What house is he in?

DECLARATIONS

DEAR MISS MANNERS—I freely admit that I am a knuckle-dragging motorcycle rider who is lacking in social graces. I lack the expertise to know how to diplomatically tell the women in my life—namely my wife, my step-daughters, my favorite aunt and my granddaughters—that I love them all.

GENTLE READER—Miss Manners doesn't know how you define social graces, but she finds you charming. Anyway, telling people you love them does not require diplomacy. You just blurt it out. It's telling them just about anything else that requires diplomacy.

LISTENING

What did you do on your summer vacation? And aren't you glad Miss Manners asked?

The suspicious reader may notice what a remarkably

short time it took Miss Manners to get from asking about you to talking about herself. That is the problem she wishes to illustrate.

Here you are, back from a holiday on which you loyally kept your dear friends constantly in mind. "That will wow them" (more likely "'em," which Miss Manners does not allow herself) you mused, as you fashioned a running commentary of what you saw and did. "Wait 'til they hear about THAT back home."

They still have not heard, although you have been home for a while. Nobody will listen. No sooner do you begin than you are stopped by one or more of the following responses:

"Yes, well, let me tell you what's been happening around HERE."

"That reminds me of what happened to me once."

"Did you eat at that little restaurant about six blocks from the town hall, with the hidden entrance to the side of the park? No? You don't know what you've missed."

"How much did you pay? Really? You should have talked to me before you went. I'm afraid you've been had."

"You should have been there before it was spoiled by the tourists. Then it was really worth going."

At this point, the returning vacationer, if easily bruised, might worry about his or her ability to plan a holiday, let alone to get two sentences out without boring people senseless. Allow Miss Manners to say reassuringly that neither of those possible defects is the trouble.

We know it wasn't boredom that estranged the listeners, because in order to be boring you have to be allowed to say something. It is true that the returned vacationer suffers from the reputation of others in the same position—

legendary figures who actually got their stories out. According to folk memory, these people did such a thorough job of numbing all their friends, with the help of postal cards, souvenirs and all manifestations of which the photographic process is capable, that they ruined in perpetuity the reputation of anyone who has ever utilized time off from work for more than mowing the lawn. These figures from the past are also said to have done their job with malicious intent. Far from wanting to share their joys and discoveries, they lived to make others feel discontent with their own lot for not having been along. Braggarts and bores may not be interchangeable, but the combination is unbeatable.

Nevertheless, Miss Manners can hardly imagine that the sins of previous generations of merrymakers are what make otherwise well-disposed friends wary of those who have been away. She suspects that the problem, rather, is that the art, or grace, of listening to long, cheerful narratives by friends or relations seems to have been lost. Before anyone blames that on the national attention span, she wishes to point out that drawn-out tragedy is politely presumed to have conversational right of way.

It may well be that the story of your bleak love life is less gripping than the story of your adventures at the beach. A report about your feelings of worthlessness is likely to be devoid of incident, while a report about your dream trip may be sparkling with it. Yet kindly people who feel obliged to listen to the former, even repeatedly and at odd hours, have little patience for the latter.

Well, vacations too need to be told. An otherwise normal person cannot be expected to disappear for a week or a month, reappear in accustomed surroundings, and not have something to tell. The mannerly person will stand still long enough to listen.

SHOWING INTEREST

Dear Miss Manners—I seem to turn people off who think I'm conceited or a know-it-all, when I'm certainly not. Neither am I dull, uninterested or lazy.

I have always known what I wanted and how to get it, and been very responsible and dependable. I got my college degree and got married when I was hardly 20 years old. I've accomplished just about all I've wanted. We started out with zero money, and now we are retired and living on the golf course in a very nice community, with savings for the rest of our lives, so we are not dependent on others.

I have been slowed down eight times with major surgery, having three children, and numerous other aches and pains, or I would have circumnavigated the world. My children are all grown, well-educated and on their own. The three grandsons are doing nicely. I just bought the children computer systems so that they can use them and teach the grandchildren.

I grow award-winning roses and am working on a novel, following a family essay done last year, and on two master's degrees.

Whenever I'm in a group, it's hard to stay silent when I've done or been what they are discussing. I'm no genius, but 200 per cent ingenuity and interest.

How can I enter into conversations without turning people off? Also, I intimidate my daughters-in-law because they can't keep up. I hate this, but then again, I'm proud of what I've accomplished and don't like them or anyone considering it all nothing. They should be proud of their great husbands! I won't let anything negative in my life and this problem bothers me.

GENTLE READER—Dear, dear. Miss Manners is pleased about your accomplishments, but she does see your problem.

Granted that you are writing to fill Miss Manners in on your background, there is still too much of you in your voice and too little of anyone else. That is what is offending people.

For example, what do you mean when you say your daughters-in-law "can't keep up"? That they are not getting double master's degrees and growing roses—or in some way patterning their lives on yours? Perhaps they have different goals, different circumstances or different levels of energy. Could you not be trying to understand what it is that they want out of life, and sympathizing with whatever difficulties they may have?

You say you are full of "interest"—which ought to mean interest in other people, especially if you wish to be a novelist. When you join conversations, do you show that interest? Miss Manners suspects you are rather tending to your interest in seeing that others do not treat your achievements "as nothing."

Don't worry about that. Your reward is the pleasure you have gotten out of life, not in impressing others. Besides, they will be twice as impressed if they find out accidentally. Those who are lucky enough to have accomplished everything they have wanted ought to have the generosity to focus on others.

CHAPTER 6

PERSONAL REMARKS
AND INQUIRIES

CONSTRUCTIVE CRITICISM

It is widely believed that we all appreciate receiving truly constructive criticism. Miss Manners never hears this declaration made more vehemently than when it comes from someone who has just received criticism and hates it.

"But this wasn't constructive," the injured party inevitably wails. "I would welcome truly constructive criticism."

This has left Miss Manners wondering exactly what the definition of constructive criticism is. Perhaps **"You do too much for others—you're just going to have to learn to let me spoil you."** Any other kind of criticism is explained as petty, self-interested, intrusive, misguided and the result not of the fault of the person criticized but of the poor digestion of the critic.

As a matter of fact, Miss Manners tends to agree with this condemnation when the subject is the sort of unsolicited, free-lance, let-me-tell-you-what's-wrong-with-your-life offering that has unfortunately become so common in modern life. The polite solution to the difficulty of accepting such criticism is for people to stop giving it.

By the way, that goes for constructive criticism too. Even when the solution is supplied, unsolicited criticism is rude. As a general rule, any sentence beginning with *"You ought to"* is going to end badly for the person addressed.

Miss Manners does recognize situations in which criticism is sought and warranted. Many of these are professional— the only person madder than an artist whose show has been reviewed badly is one whose show hasn't been reviewed at all. Some, however, are personal—when advice has either been sincerely and actively sought, or is offered with the confidence that the closeness of the relationship warrants suggesting a reasonable and limited change.

Even that requires extreme delicacy of manners. It is said that dispensing advice is easy. What is difficult is getting anyone to listen to it.

Miss Manners proposes a polite and therefore effective procedure for offering criticism that she picked up from a playwriting group attended by a gentleman of her acquaintance. The fact of belonging to a group whose primary purpose is the exchange of useful criticism would not, Miss Manners ventures, make criticism easier to take. That the criticism is a professional matter, not a personal one—the social rule of "If you can't say anything good, don't say anything" wouldn't be very useful—does not make it potentially less damaging.

There are two rules in this group. One is that the session following the reading of a play, when the playwright faces his peers, is opened by a group leader who says, **"First, let's hear what works in this play. What did you like?"** Only after the good points have been produced and discussed does the leader say, **"And now let's talk about what doesn't work."**

The second rule is that no one is allowed to tell the playwright what he should do with the play. You can't rewrite someone else's play, is the way it is put. This of course eliminates a great deal of that constructive part of constructive criticism—the part that says, "Actually, if I had done this, I would have done it better."

These two rules, Miss Manners wishes to point out, also apply to criticism made about personal matters.

First, a statement of approval properly paves the way for a specific complaint. This is not done to flatter the subject into thinking that everything is all right before the whammy is delivered, so much as to say that the criticism is nothing basic. It is but one flaw among many virtues. Whether or not this is strictly true, it makes criticism more effective, as well as palatable. To work on changing one thing may seem worthwhile, but major overhauls seem hopeless.

Second, no one really does have the ability to tell another how to live his or her life. Miss Manners realizes that believing so is what makes criticizing others such a popular sport. Perhaps they would be better employed in rewriting their own plays.

UNSOLICITED ADVICE

DEAR MISS MANNERS—I have an urge to make a suggestion to a good friend of mine, but I am not certain whether this would offend her.

She is a beautiful person, both inside and out. However, I would love to see her wear some makeup, even if it is a small amount of lipstick, and perhaps style her long hair. She is a very shy person about her looks and tends to hide them. I think she should stop this nonsense and show people how beautiful she really is. With a slight change, she might feel more confident about her self-image. Should I keep my comments to myself?

GENTLE READER—Probably. If you have noticed how beautiful your friend is, Miss Manners imagines that others have too. That her beauty would be enhanced by cosmetics and hair styling is merely your opinion, with which others may not concur.

One of those others is your friend. It is hardly imaginable that in this day and age, she is not aware that artificial beauty aids are available to those who want them. Telling someone she needs them is hardly likely to add to her confidence. This cannot help but make her realize that you, for one, find her appearance unsatisfactory.

However, you notice that Miss Manners hedged a bit by saying "probably" rather than "absolutely not." She is not totally opposed to the exchange of advice, provided it is done by close friends, which you say you are, with some humility and tact.

She will therefore allow you to ask your friend, apparently idly, if she has ever tried playing around with makeup and hairstyles, and whether she would enjoy doing so with you. If she shows interest, you might then offer suggestions, always for her judgment; but if she doesn't, you must let it pass. If you want to enhance her confidence, you might try telling her that you find her beautiful.

COMPLAINING

DEAR MISS MANNERS—How does one (politely) tell another associate that he/she is applying far too much aftershave/perfume?

Associates who work near these people have suffered cases of tearing eyes and breathing difficulty. Our "offenders," one man, one woman, obviously bathe daily, and they both dress to the proverbial nines. We are fully confident that they are not trying to hide bad hygiene, but merely do not recognize the potency of their applied fragrances.

We love both of these people dearly and do not wish to hurt their feelings. We just can't seem to find a method for communicating our problem without causing a painful situation.

Would you be most gracious and provide us your answer before some thoughtless clod (we have some of those here too) speaks up?

GENTLE READER—From a file bulging with letters complaining about the personal habits of coworkers, Miss Manners decided to use yours because:

1. The problem you describe is not one that would interfere with anyone's breakfast just hearing about it. The catalogue of other smells and sights of which office workers complain is unpleasantly amazing in its variety.

2. It was graciously put. The thoughtless clod approach, which assumes that the offenders are not just oblivious but indifferent to the effect they produce, and that it could best be brought to their attention through ridicule and insult, is common.

3. It's easy to solve, because the offending element was artificially applied, rather than emanating from the body, the latter route being something people take a bit more personally than the former.

The task is best done by an extremely close friend or, one might say, the opposite—a supervisor. There are different methods for each, and while neither is anyone's idea of fun, there are different delicacies permitted.

A close friend (who has to be a lot closer than a merely friendly colleague) can sniff the air and (talking from the assumption of his or her general affection and admiration for the person) say, **"I don't know if you realize how strong that scent is—you should use it more sparingly."** This has the advantage of not revealing that the error has attracted the awareness and distaste of others.

In contrast, a supervisor can disassociate him- or herself from the complaint, even to the extent of seeming unsure whether it applies to that particular worker: **"There have been some complaints from people who are having bad reactions to the use of cologne—if this applies to you, I'd appreciate it if you'd cut back on it."**

Notice that both methods become a lot harder when it is not perfumes that are involved. This is when Miss Manners would like to remind people of the value of that much-maligned institution, the euphemism. Those who brag bravely that they always deal in undisguised bluntness rightly falter when it comes to naming such names.

Thus, body odor becomes "reaction to the heat in here." And anything to do with the nose becomes vaguely, if inaccurately, attributed to colds, allergies or sinus trouble.

COMPLAINING ABOUT SMOKE

DEAR MISS MANNERS—I find it rude when another person starts smoking close to me in an enclosed public building. If that person wants to ruin their body, that's fine, but they don't have to ruin mine, too. I've found that coughing loudly or stage whispering to a friend how I can't breathe usually works, but I don't believe that is the best way to solve the problem.

GENTLE READER—No, and you'll be amazed at what the best way is. It involves the assumption of goodwill on the part of a fellow human being.

Yes! Even one who smokes! The polite way to ask someone not to smoke in your presence is to say "**Excuse me, but I'm afraid smoke bothers me.**"

Miss Manners is not promising that it will always work. You may have to send for someone who will invoke rules against smoking in the building—or, if the rule doesn't apply, avoid the area. But a polite start at least offers the smoker a less embarrassing chance to apologize and put out the cigarette or smoke elsewhere than does an amateur dramatization of impending death from secondhand smoke.

UNSOLICITED INFORMATION

DEAR MISS MANNERS—It seems that whenever I eat something, people feel it is their duty to inform me of how much fat/calories or cholesterol is in these items.

I have never had a problem with cholesterol or gaining weight. In fact, I am healthy and very near my ideal weight. How should I reply to these constant unsolicited remarks?

GENTLE READER—"**Want some?**"

FAMILIARITY

"Wow!" said the waiter. *"I saw you this afternoon when you and your friend came in and made your reservation, and I guess you went home and fixed yourself up. It's a big improvement."*

"Finished already!" said another waiter in another restau-

rant. *"You people really eat fast. I was just coming by to check how you were getting along, and you're already finished with your appetizers."*

"Where are you folks from?" a waitress in yet a third restaurant asked the couple who had sneaked away to be alone. *"Been here before?"*

All of these restaurant-goers reported being rattled by the unexpected attention. Although they had meant to step into the public arena, they hadn't quite counted on being observed and evaluated so frankly. They all resolved not to go back for another such appraisal.

Miss Manners does not believe that people who have the difficult job of recommending and hauling food, hours at a stretch, for often finicky and snippy customers, have any ruder impulses than anyone else. Nor does she suspect them of having an inordinate interest in other people's business. Although these incidents happened in restaurants, the problem is one that pervades society, affecting not only the conversational styles of a wide range of businesses, but social life as well.

Etiquette books used to identify this etiquette violation as "familiarity," meaning the unwarranted assumption of intimacy. But the warnings against it ceased when the poor etiquetteers became terrified of the charge of snobbery, itself an etiquette violation, which Miss Manners has no intention of committing.

Back in those not-so-good-old days, familiarity was perceived as an offense that could be committed only by people taking liberties with their supposed betters. The concept of low-ranking people—service people, children—not knowing their proper place was and is an offensive one in a republic.

The much greater problem, of the so-called betters being

overly familiar to those not in a good position to complain, was ignored. The customer who wished to press personal attentions on a waitress, for example, was considered to be displaying mere joviality, not what we would now properly identify as harassment.

Miss Manners would like to point out that the pretense of intimacy among strangers in a business association—no matter what their hierarchical positions relative to one another—can be seriously annoying to either side. Why, then, is it not only more and more usual, but often vehemently defended?

The answer has to do with our noble commitment to egalitarianism, and a mistaken notion that it necessarily precludes privacy. Among equals, are we not all friends?

Well, no. Equals get to choose their friends, and while most people enjoy a cheerful demeanor while transacting the commercial details of daily life, not everyone wants to extend the privileges of friendship under those circumstances.

This is by no means to say that many restaurant patrons, for example, are not gratified to be recognized at places they customarily patronize, and to engage in such pleasantries as asking after one another's health or family. The point about such chatting, as in such other contacts between strangers as conversations on trains or airplanes, is that it be agreeable to both sides, and that it not assume the prerogatives of those who are on truly familiar terms.

Even among friends and relatives, the boundaries of privacy are dangerously imperceptible to many people these days. You probably do not want your intimates to offer critical appraisals of your appearance or your eating habits, or to make you account for all your comings and goings. So you are not likely to want to pay for such services either.

NAMES

Dear Miss Manners—As an addition to the running discourse on the practice of calling strangers by their first names, you might be interested in a conversation I overheard while getting my driver's license recently.

The clerk called the man in the next lane who was applying for his license by his first name, and he replied very politely, **"Is my last name too difficult for you?"** It was a simple one; Cromwell, I believe.

Gentle Reader—Please present Miss Manners' compliments to Mr. Cromwell, should you see him again. Presuming that he made his statement in a polite voice, she congratulates him for refusing to accept cheekiness from strangers. She also hopes he got his license.

CONSTRUCTIVE REACTIONS

How obligated is the polite person to assist those less fortunate in the way of manners to get their feet out of their mouths?

The question was raised when a gentleman of Miss Manners' acquaintance asked how best to lessen the embarrassment of a stranger who had asked him whether he was the grandfather of toddlers who were, in fact, his children. What he wanted to discuss was whether it was necessary to conceal the truth of the situation for the sake of the stranger's feelings, perhaps at the risk of hopelessly confusing his children.

Miss Manners wanted to discuss something else. It seemed to her that politeness required him to refrain from responding peevishly, but that it did not oblige him to protect people from the consequences of their own transgressions.

We can probably assume that the inquiry as to the relationship between this gentleman and young children in his charge was not maliciously meant, and, in fact, there was no hurt inflicted.

But there might have been. Miss Manners has heard from more than one mature mother who has resented a similar inquiry, and a young one equally annoyed at being asked "Is that your sister?" The intrusiveness of guessing other people's circumstances is neither necessary nor excusable.

Here is a selection of complaints Miss Manners has received from people who were hurt by questions and comments from those who would doubtless maintain that they were innocently being friendly:

"I know exactly where my biological mother lives and could see her at any time, but I don't wish to. So I don't appreciate questions like, *'Have you ever seen your "real" mother?'* or inquiries about the events that led to my adoption. I know these people don't mean to be cruel, but even after you're grown-up, there's still a little soft spot about being 'real,' and it doesn't help if someone asks if you think your parents love you as much as if you'd been born to them."

"My fiancé and I have been engaged for some months now, and will marry in a few more. Friends we don't see on a day-to-day basis often inquire, *'So—are you still getting married?'* They have no reason to think otherwise, and the implication that our engagement is not serious is rankling."

"For reasons I am too much of a lady to discuss, I had my tubes tied. Am I required to explain my reasons for this elective surgery when people ask aloud, *'But why?'*"

"After our first child was born prematurely and died, and a second stressful but normal pregnancy, our beautiful daughter was born 15 months ago. I am beset daily by inquiring minds—*'When are you going to have another one?'* or *'It's about time for another one, isn't it?'* I would love to reply, 'It's none of your business,' but these are not meddlesome busybodies who deserve a slap in the face, just well-meaning co-workers who need a gentle reminder of proper manners."

"An acquaintance is fond of asking *'How much did you pay for this?'* and *'Did your father help you pay for that?'* Being an adult on my own for more than 20 years, I view as an insult the implication that I am not able to support myself."

Here are three polite ways of making it clear that a question is not welcome:

Treat it as if the proper thing had been said: **"Thank you, I know I have your good wishes."**

Acknowledge the curiosity without satisfying it: **"Thank you for taking an interest."**

Say something irrelevant: **"They are wonderful children."**

Kindly said, none of these replies should humiliate the person who has carelessly crossed the line from interest to nosiness. But if it suggests to that person that exercising more consideration in the future would be a good idea, Miss Manners would not be sorry.

COUNTERING ORDINARY ASSUMPTIONS

DEAR MISS MANNERS—I'm single now, in my 50's, and recently had the dreadful experience of attending my 40th high school reunion. I look wonderful and healthy and am much happier once I recovered from an ugly divorce after a 31 year marriage. I had expected to have a good time.

I did not. Out of 100 classmates, the majority were married and still in the first marriage. That's good. But here is what I got:

"Hi, where's your husband?"
"Oh, a divorce, how sad."
"Don't worry, you'll get a man."

It wasn't nice or funny—it hurt—and it got real old when repeated about 20 times. How about a verbal kick to smug married attitudes toward single people in general, women over 50 in particular? My reply was a lewd look and a comment that I was happy, and then an exit from their company.

GENTLE READER—Miss Manners does not normally congratulate ladies on issuing lewd looks, but you seem to have handled an awkward situation satisfactorily.

Certainly people make an extraordinary number of stupidly tactless remarks these days, as Miss Manners keeps more or less gently pointing out to them. Ever since the idea got around that self-expression was an unmitigated virtue, not to be hampered by mere considerations of etiquette (such as how it makes the hearer feel), there has been a veritable flood of such statements. But let us distinguish between what is awful to say, and what is awful to hear. They are not necessarily the same thing.

"Don't worry, you'll get a man" is offensive to anyone, at any time, under any circumstances. No contest there.

But "Where's your husband?" is a conventionally innocent social remark that has only recently turned dangerous. Inquiring after people's families is polite, rather than the reverse. It is only as divorce has become rampant that cautious people have stopped assuming that spouses are permanent family, rather than privileged transients.

A widow would be in a position similar to yours, in recognizing the necessity of giving old acquaintances news that might be painful to repeat. But one would not expect people to avoid all mention of spouses on the grounds that no one lives forever.

You need only have replied **"We are no longer married,"** with further discussion optional. Any inquiries can be met with a pleasant but firm **"I would prefer not to discuss it."**

The borderline case here is commiserating over a divorce. No matter how joyful some people may feel at being released, a divorce is nevertheless the failure of a marriage. One cannot expect the conventional **"I'm sorry,"** used when one knows nothing of the circumstances, to be changed to an all-purpose "Good for you."

CONSIDERING MOTIVATION

DEAR MISS MANNERS—Two people can always be counted upon to ask me about "boyfriends" or "dating." One is my father's first cousin, a man now in his 70s. The other is a close girlfriend and former college roommate. I see these people (separately) once a year at most, but the problem irritates me every time.

The first time my cousin inquired in a loudly cheerful voice, *"Well, and how about the boyfriends?"* I, who was not involved with anyone then and had not been for years, mumbled some sort of embarrassed response. Looking back later, I became angry, feeling I owed nobody an explanation or justification of my social life.

The following year, in the presence of his wife and a handful of our relatives, he posed the same question. I responded by saying, "If there's anyone worth mentioning, I'll bring him into the conversation." I thought this a tactful way of telling him if there was news, he would get it without asking. A few minutes later, he observed that I had brought no one into the conversation. Where do we go from there?

The girlfriend, a physician, will ask me if I have been dating—employing the same tone my dentist uses when asking whether I have been flossing. Perhaps this is automatic in her profession. Should I explain that the implied condescension strikes me as inappropriate?

Our perplexing encounters with college men were a topic of absorbing interest when we were sophomores and living in a girls' dormitory. But that was in the spring of 1965. I would like to think the passage of that much time has brought more than morning stiffness and the need for bifocals. My present situation adds a complicating element, as an intense relationship which lasted for over a year is in the process of disintegration. I do not wish to offer a simplistic, finger-pointing explanation, nor to produce a detailed analysis. How does one deal honestly, without waxing heavy-handed or sarcastic, with a probing one considers an invasion of privacy?

GENTLE READER—While inquiring about romance is always nosy, these superficially identical probings are inspired by different motivations, so slightly different remedies are in order.

Cousin Herman just wants to make conversation. He believes that young ladies, which is to say ladies younger than he is, are only interested in boys and clothes, and he doesn't know how to talk about clothes. All you need say is **"Oh, Cousin Herman, you know I'm waiting for someone just like you,"** if you then go on to open a conversation on a topic of interest to him.

Your friend, however, dates from the time when you did want to talk about boys, if not clothes. (The therapeutic tone that you say your college friend takes also offends Miss Manners, but unless she comes out and says that falling in love would be good for your liver, let us ignore that.) She is not out of line in presuming the old level of confidences unless you indicate otherwise. The way to do that is to say, cheerfully, **"Oh, Miranda, men come and go, God bless them, but I just can't have as much fun gossiping about them as we used to in school. Tell me what you've been doing."**

KEEPING A SECRET

DEAR MISS MANNERS—I'm dating a very nice gentleman. Our public behavior is always discreet. Twice we have been asked publicly, i.e., in social settings with many other people present, if we are dating, married, etc. Each time we have smiled courteously and said dating, then changed the subject. Can you suggest a polite way to indicate that the question is rude and inappropriate?

GENTLE READER—The phrase you are looking for is **"We are just good friends."** Since it offers less information than either of the choices with which you were so rudely presented, it has the advantage of infuriating the questioner.

MAINTAINING SILENCE

DEAR MISS MANNERS—How does one politely respond to a stranger asking, *"Have you accepted Christ?"*—particularly if the individual is installed in the neighboring seat on the Metro?

GENTLE READER—This does not happen to be on Miss Manners' list of questions from strangers that one is obligated to answer on public transportation. Those questions are: **"Could you please tell me the time?" "Excuse me, but what stop is this?"** and, lately, **"Does anybody have change of a dollar?"**

All other questions may be answered with a vague, puzzled, silent smile, after which one returns to the staring-straight-ahead, absorbed-in-thought posture that makes city life feasible for those who do not want to pass their entire lives baring their souls to strangers.

REFUSING TO REACT

DEAR MISS MANNERS—Please advise a suitable response (one hopefully with an edge) to the question *"When do you plan to retire?"*

I am a gainfully employed, energetic, competent, hard working employee, and also quite youthful for my years. I have no intention of retiring before my time, but am really weary of this infernal, rude question.

GENTLE READER—Miss Manners presumes it is neither your boss nor your assistant who is asking the question.

As a social query, it is rude, she agrees. But one may assume that someone who asks it doesn't think so—is, indeed, ready to discuss his or her own retirement. So while Miss Manners doesn't know about edges, she would countenance your replying, **"I haven't begun to think about it. What about you?"**

RESPONDING TO RUDENESS

THE GRACEFUL RETREAT

Here are some sample exchanges on the subject of etiquette. Miss Manners regrets to say that they come from everyday life—commonness is exactly what they most have in common.

Some of the people involved believe themselves to be guardians of etiquette. Others claim they care nothing about etiquette, but just want other people to behave right, which is nevertheless a pretty good definition of etiquette.

He: *"You want me to ram your car? I saw this space first."*
She: *"Go ahead and try it. I'll have you in jail so fast you won't know what hit you."*

She: *"Take your filthy habit somewhere else, you're making me sick."*
He: *"Yeah? I'm staying right here. But you want to know where you can go?"*

He: *"You busted in line. We all saw you, so you can get out right now and wait your turn like the rest of us."*
She: *"I've got just as much right to be here as you."*

She: *"Hey, move it! We got here an hour ago, and you're blocking my little boy's view."*
He: *"Who's going to make me, you or the kid?"*

Miss Manners' question is: Can you identify the rude-nesses in these exchanges?

The people quoted certainly can. Each of them claims it is the other who was rude—the first speakers in each exchange, because they recognized rude acts (and merely retaliated); and the second, because they recognized rude remarks (and merely retaliated).

So we have matched pairs of antagonists, both of whom claim to be the victims of rudeness, and both of whom are inordinately proud of taking a stand against bad be-havior.

Frankly, Miss Manners sees nothing but rudeness on both sides. Furthermore, the scenes don't improve as they develop, which is why she cut them off after the openings. Once the barrier of etiquette has been smashed, she doesn't care to stick around for the ensuing violence.

What puzzles her is how the participants manage to believe that they are advancing the cause of politeness. Has either side convinced the other of the folly of being rude? As a result of these exchanges, will there be less rudeness with which either party has to contend in the future? Perhaps this all-important issue tends to get lost in the melee. All parties may boast instead that the important thing is that they feel better after having given vent to their feelings.

But Miss Manners' concern has never been the airing of unpleasantness that, in turn, pollutes the air. She would like to stick to the question of how to avoid both kinds of unpleasantness—the rude act and the rude rejoinder—so that the question of spewing venom to get rid of bitterness does not even come up.

To begin with, she does not disagree about the offensiveness of the provoking acts. But motivation counts in judging etiquette disputes, and it is by no means always clear that such acts were intentional. In any case, to treat offenses as accidents gives the offenders a face-saving way to back down from them.

Such statements as **"Excuse me, but I believe I was here first"** and **"I don't believe that's permitted here"** can, if uttered in the tone of sympathetic regret, permit the response of **"Oh, sorry, I didn't realize that,"** accompanied by a retreat. There is no need to defend one's erroneous stance, because one hasn't been attacked for it.

You say you tried it, and it didn't work? No, because Miss Manners heard the sarcasm in your voice. Try it again, first working yourself up to a belief in the assumption of innocence.

Miss Manners herself has had a remarkable success rate with this practice, not only because she genuinely believes in the possibility of the accidental violation, but because she believes in the essential reasonableness and fairness of humanity. Appealed to in that spirit, a remarkable number of people who have been identified as relentlessly rude take advantage of the graceful retreat she offers them. So even if Miss Manners did not ban rudeness as a response to rudeness, she would have to point out that politeness has a higher success rate.

REJECTING NICENESS

DEAR MISS MANNERS—Is there a training class for ladies too gently bred?

Salespeople address me as Hon or Honey. I sometimes seem invisible—people walk right into me. Sometimes I feel like opening the window and screaming, *"I'm mad as hell!"* but I doubt anyone would notice. I should have realized how life was to be when I was in kindergarten. All of the children were lined up to get shots. All were screaming except me. All the screamers were given pieces of candy. I got none.

GENTLE READER—Is it too late for Miss Manners to offer you candy? She desperately wants to keep you from finding those training classes which—by substituting such names as "assertiveness" as euphemisms for rudeness—do indeed exist to turn gentle people rough. But do you really feel you need to add yourself to the number of screamers in the world? Would it even help? You are quite right in believing that no one would notice your screaming in the general din.

However, the choice between being a rude success and a polite victim is a false one. Etiquette is not without its polite defenses, and they are often more effective than retaliatory rudeness. Miss Manners can understand that a child would not think of saying "I would like a candy, too, please," and deplores the callousness that created the situation you describe. But surely you are old enough now to say, firmly, **"That's 'Ma'am,' not 'Hon,' if you please."**

POINTING OUT GUILT

DEAR MISS MANNERS—People who cheat think that others have an obligation to allow them to do so, and resent anyone who calls them on it. Many times when I am in the supermarket fast lane, with its posted limit of ten items, people will unload well over ten items and everyone there, including the checker, will allow these cheats and bullies to get away with it rather than incur their wrath.

But I think that it is a matter of fairness and I speak up, whereupon the person (and sometimes everyone there) acts as if it is rude, or being a snitch. I just think it is cowardly to let people get away with cheating and that this just encourages them to continue. I think that rules should apply equally to all.

GENTLE READER—So does Miss Manners. She carries this to the extreme extent of believing that that pesky rule about not using rudeness to counteract rudeness applies to such worthy citizens as yourself and herself.

She does not mind your snitching to do your moral duty. But denouncing people as bullies or cheats, or even questioning their fairness, is rude.

Polite snitching assumes that the violator has entered the line mistakenly. If you say pleasantly, but pointedly, **"Excuse me, but this is the express line; I think you want the other cashier,"** you allow a face-saving retreat. Even the brazen back off when everybody in a line turns to watch. What's more, you may actually have encountered an honest mistake. Even moral people are required to follow that nuisance of a rule about assuming people innocent.

SHOCK

DEAR MISS MANNERS—Is there any gracious way to prevent people from assuming that my boyfriend and I sleep together?

One of my few successes followed my introduction to a local priest as "X's girlfriend." The priest joked about "wife" and "girlfriend" being all the same nowadays, but when I mumbled "not really" and blushed in discomfort, he was gracious enough to blush an eloquent apology at his mistaken assumption.

Others have been less willing to part with their assumptions. Human nature seems to favor jumping to conclusions and to resist correction. I suppose the problem is theirs, not mine, yet their assumptions leave me uncomfortable.

I have no need or desire to judge others who believe differently, but I highly value marriage as a unique and special commitment of intimacy and trust, which is well worth abstinence in the meantime, and I want to be a clear witness to my values. Statements such as "My boyfriend and I do not have intercourse" or "We're saving ourselves for marriage" seem preachy, uncomfortably intimate conversation stoppers. Yet this is such an apparently revolutionary concept that any less direct attempts are futile.

GENTLE READER—You were insulted in church by a priest who thinks it funny to assume that what he once called "living in sin" is now the standard of his congregation?

Where are Miss Manners' smelling salts?

Miss Manners trusts that this incident will have plunged the priest into some serious soul-searching as to why he has turned what presumably started as tolerance of human weakness into abandonment of higher standards. Personally, she has always been wary of clergy who use the word "nowadays" too often, whether humorously or angrily. Aren't they supposed to recognize a force even more august than peer pressure?

Blushing is hardly a sufficient apology for an unwarranted attack on the honor of a lady, by a priest or anyone else. But

Miss Manners understands that while you wish to reject these assumptions, you do not want to preach to others. (We know whose department that is, don't we?) There is a nonarrogant way of looking shocked, which is what Miss Manners presumes you did naturally—and successfully—in the encounter you described.

"Oh, no, we're not married" is the proper reply to the question of whether you and your boyfriend live together. Should anyone rudely persist by claiming that most couples do, you need only remark **"Really!"** This indicates that one need not be naive not to take advantage of the lax standards of others.

A SHOCKING RESPONSE

DEAR MISS MANNERS—When someone tells me I have gray hair or that I've gained some weight, I'm usually too shocked at their remarks to say anything. I would like to let these people know how distasteful their comments are, without being reduced to their level.

GENTLE READER—Miss Manners recommends: **"Oh, thank you; how kind of you to notice."** She has found that it is the one remark that can shock such people.

A SATISFYING RESPONSE

DEAR MISS MANNERS—I am a 52-year-old woman, but I really do not show my age—I am slim, elegant, and take good care of myself. But at a party, one of the guests said, in front of several people, *"When I get old, I want to look like Maggie."*

She is 44 years old, and to be honest she looks older than I do. I was so shocked that I did not know what to say. Should I have taken her remark as a compliment, or what would be the better answer to such uncalled-for rudeness?

GENTLE READER—Miss Manners does not allow you to retaliate for rudeness with rudeness, but she does not mind a politely delivered response with just the hint of a zinger in it. You could say, kindly, **"Oh, but my dear, you have such a long way to go."**

OUTRAGE

DEAR MISS MANNERS—What is a racist? How does one respond when charged with racism? Is there a defense, or is it like medieval witchcraft? If you float you're a witch? If you drown, you might have been innocent, but at least you're not a problem any more.

The people who make these accusations have no interest in my fate, but the question being raised, even without evidence, jeopardizes my career. Can you help? I consider myself a fair person, but I'm truly disturbed and feel completely defenseless.

GENTLE READER—Miss Manners can only imagine the agonizing situation that prompts you to ask such a question. Obviously, she is in no position to judge the charge that was made.

But she has noticed that some people now make such charges almost casually, without taking the full responsibility of staining someone's honor. Accusing someone of being a racist—or of being a liar or a thief—is so serious that it is only excusable when the accuser is prepared to offer firm evidence to substantiate the charge.

However the charge is made, it must be taken seriously by the accused. The defense is to express outrage, to make a counteraccusation that one has been slandered, and to demand that the evidence be aired in front of whoever has heard the accusation.

Miss Manners is sorry to incite you to confrontation. It is necessary because traditionally, the act of swallowing an insult has been considered tantamount to admitting that it is true.

BANISHMENT

DEAR MISS MANNERS—At a cocktail party I gave, a rather close friend brought one of his friends, who wandered about telling everyone how much he hated my furniture and generally made fun of everything. I didn't say anything at the time, but afterward told my friend not to bring him into my home again. Is it ever acceptable simply to ask someone to leave for acting like a clueless jerk?

GENTLE READER—No, but it is gracious to release one who does not seem to be enjoying the occasion. You could have produced his coat saying, **"I'm so sorry you're not happy here; I wouldn't dream of keeping you."**

IN LIEU OF DUELING

DEAR MISS MANNERS—I am an only child, and find it very rude when people who don't even know me tell me I am spoiled. My friends who know me very well don't think I am spoiled, but when someone who has just met me hears I don't have any brothers or sisters, they make comments I find insulting. Is there anything I can do or say that would stop people from acting like this?

GENTLE READER You are right to be insulted, and Miss Manners trusts you will not allow such people to talk you into the idea that they are offering you helpful psychological insights. She finds it outrageous that people go about nowadays casually saying things that would, in bygone days, lead to duels.

As we no longer have the duel as a defense, you have the choice of saying "How dare you?" or "Why, thank you." Miss Manners recommends the latter. The former would probably lead such people into an insulting discussion of your "hostility," which is the way such people describe a self-respecting reaction to insult. An unexpected and undeserved **"Thank you,"** delivered with a cold look, calls attention to their rudeness in an impeccable, and therefore more effective, way.

DEALING WITH THE ETIQUETTE–CHALLENGED

DEAR MISS MANNERS—I have a beautiful, intelligent, sociable, nine-month-old daughter who also happens to have spina bifida. While my husband and I admit that her condition is an inconvenience, we consider ourselves very fortunate indeed to be her parents. We hope that she will grow up feeling the same way about her condition—that it is an inconvenience, and nothing more.

How does one handle public displays of pity? For

example, I had her picture taken today, and I had to tell the photographer about her paralysis so that he could position her for the portrait. He kept saying, *"Poor baby."* I worry about the day when she will be old enough to understand such comments, and that when she gets her wheelchair, they will become frequent.

I understand that people are sympathetic, but I am not sure that pity has a place in our society today. We have come to expect people to function to the best of their abilities, regardless of their limitations. In order to do that, handicapped persons must have a positive attitude, a good self-image, and a feeling of pride in what they can accomplish. I feel that public displays of pity hinder the development of these qualities.

Can you provide me with one of your trademark polite, succinct and effective rejoinders? I would love to hear someone say, "Well, she certainly is a beautiful child; you must be very proud"—because I am.

GENTLE READER—Of course you are, and Miss Manners has noticed that you don't need any special help from her to say so. You articulate your maternal pride, as well as your maternal wisdom, eloquently indeed.

So she will only attempt to help you condense it for the sort of brief, annoying encounters you describe. Your daughter will soon pick up your tone, which will be valuable when she has to deal with pitying comments on her own, so you should make sure it doesn't sound defensive.

At this point, you should just seem incredulous when you say **"What on earth do you mean? She's a wonderful child!"** firmly enough to stave off further discussion. As she gets older, you can allow yourself a satisfied little laugh as you say **"Poor child? The person I feel sorry for is anyone who is silly enough to underestimate her."**

FORBEARANCE

DEAR MISS MANNERS—On a recent business trip, I invited a work colleague and his wife to dinner. During the conversation, she asked to see a picture of my four-month baby girl. As she was looking at the snapshot, she said, *"Oh, she doesn't look like a day care baby."* As you can tell, this lady stays home with her children full-time.

Since your advice is usually not to respond to rudeness with more rudeness, I said nothing. My friends tell me I should have responded shocked, insulted, or with a very sarcastic remark. Although I doubt this will happen again, what would your response have been?

GENTLE READER—Miss Manners hears the air crackling with cracks that you might have offered in exchange for this rudeness, and also with the counterattacks they might inspire. But in addition to her ban against even provoked rudeness, she has a special distaste for sparring that suggests that there is only one way for a good mother to order her life.

Therefore, Miss Manners would have restrained an admittedly strong temptation to make a fight over it, and said, gently, **"I do the best I can by her, and as you can see, she's a very happy baby."**

On the off chance that the unfortunate remark was prompted by ignorance, this would supply new evidence. Even if it had been prompted by malice, surely the example of forbearance should have reproved the offender in a way that unpleasantness could not.

AUTO–INSULT

DEAR MISS MANNERS—I am fairly thin, and I exercise to stay in shape. But I am certainly not perfect. In light conversation, people say things like, *"I am so heavy I can't buy any new things,"* or *"If I was thin like you, I could wear outfits like that."*

When the other person really does need to lose weight or shouldn't wear certain things, I never know the right thing to say. I feel that if I don't say anything, I am agreeing with them. What is a correct response that doesn't hurt their feelings, even though what they are saying might be true?

GENTLE READER—If people are going to insult themselves, Miss Manners understands the temptation to let them. But, like you, she will rise above it.

Your reply should be a nonspecific **"I think you look wonderful."** Look them smilingly in the eye when you say this, to indicate that the comment refers to the overall effect they make, not to how much they fill out their overalls.

SARCASM

DEAR MISS MANNERS—Now that I am retired, I have time to attend senior citizen functions. There is always a line for food, handouts, etc. and when I am at the end of the line, the person who should be behind me stands next to me and then, at some point, cuts in front of me. I really don't care if I am number 25 or 26, but this seems so rude. What, if anything, should I say to this person?

GENTLE READER—**"Oh, please go ahead. I'm in no hurry."** Miss Manners advises you to say this in a pleasant voice, but a loud one.

THREATS

DEAR MISS MANNERS—I live in the inner city. When I tell suburbanites and outer city residents where I live, they often ask, *"Is it safe there?"* Am I wrong to find this question insulting? Is there a correct response?

GENTLE READER—Miss Manners is always pleased to hear from a neighbor. The reply she prefers is a gentle **"Don't worry, I won't hurt you."**

CHAPTER 8

THE USE AND ABUSE
OF HUMOR

ETIQUETTE AND HUMOR

When etiquette is accused of humorlessness, it pouts.

Did you think it should laugh? As most people learn by the second grade, it is a mistake to pretend to be amused when you are ridiculed. It only encourages more of the same.

Anyway, the charge is unfair. Etiquette has plenty of uses for humor. It's just that amusement doesn't happen to be one of them. Fortunately, there is nothing unseemly about having a jolly time discouraging humor. Among the jokes Miss Manners gleefully proscribes are:

Anything based on the name of any person present, especially if it contains a pun.

Satirizing another person's appearance, such as asking silly questions about being tall, blond or fat.

The suggestion that there is something off-putting about someone's occupation, especially if it features mock fear of being attacked, caught, fooled or intellectually bested.

All kidding about the advantages the other person must have from being rich, young or otherwise privileged or protected.

It is not on the tender grounds that such joshing might damage feelings that Miss Manners insists on these rules. It is on the grounds of unbearable tedium. If you were a six-foot heiress and police officer named Rich, how many times do you think you could stand being asked how the weather was up there, whether you were born Rich and how many people at the party you were planning to arrest?

Naturally, Miss Manners also bans jokes that are based on meanness and bigotry. As a number of people have pointed out, this leaves nothing left to laugh at. If you can't go around insulting people wholesale, they argue, life is hardly worth living. Miss Manners will leave them to the company they deserve—the equally mean-spirited people who manage to find insult in every ordinary remark—and turn to the positive uses that etiquette has for humor. These come under two categories: "I Was Only Kidding" and "You Must Be Kidding." Properly used, both are indispensable to ensuring a peaceful society—so of course people have found ways to use both of them improperly.

I Was Only Kidding is the social equivalent of the insanity defense—used to nullify the possibility of evil intent from dreadful words. It should be accompanied by a look of horror and a hand clapped to the mouth to convey the notion that what everybody heard was not what one was really saying.

The popular sport of blaming others for one's mistakes has preempted this phrase for the purpose of showing that anyone who takes offense at offensiveness is at fault for not enjoying it, as one would clearly do if one had a sense of humor. It is therefore necessary for the contrite to vary the wording: "Oh, my goodness, I was trying to make a joke and it came out all wrong—please believe me that I meant nothing of the kind."

You Must Be Kidding is not, as many now seem to believe, the correct response to tragedy, as in "Your mother was run over by a bus? You must be kidding." Nor is it permissible to use the fancy wording, "Surely you jest," now that everyone has learned to reply, "I never jest, and my name's not Shirley."

It has become an attitude, rather than a statement—the position, in the face of evidence to the contrary, that an unacceptable remark must have been intended as a joke. It therefore seeks to defuse the situation by responding not with return hostilities, but with a continuation of the joke. Provided, of course, that you can discover any small topic for a joke that Miss Manners has not yet gotten around to banning.

MAKING A JOKE OF IT

DEAR MISS MANNERS—My mother-in-law and I get along superbly, and I think the world of her, but she has this habit of bringing up my husband's (her son's) past relationships with old girlfriends, going into explicit detail, describing his preferences in women and how the girls in his past pursued him.

She hasn't done this once or twice, which I could live with, but many more times than I could count. It's only when there's an audience—parties, picnics, family get-togethers. Everyone looks at me, as if waiting for a reaction, but I only sit and listen, as it wouldn't be polite to do otherwise.

My husband is never the instigator of these conversations, and I don't blame him. If you suggest he say something to her—he has, and it doesn't stop her. My in-laws are extremely aggressive and say and do whatever they want, regardless of the situation.

I realize that everyone has a past. I, too, have an interesting one, but my mother has never mentioned details, and probably never will, as she wouldn't want my husband to be uncomfortable. I can't help but wonder how my mother-in-law might feel if someone's mother did this to her own daughter.

Am I wrong to be disturbed? I pride myself on knowing my place and being mindful of others' feelings, and I wouldn't want to do anything to ruin our relationship. I chalk it up to ignorance, but how do I handle it?

GENTLE READER—Miss Manners is not so sure she chalks this up to ignorance, especially since appeals from the gentleman in question have been ignored by his own mother. But she doesn't want to spoil your generous attitude by speculating about how it could be characterized.

Let's just put a stop to it. We can't have you being subjected to this provocation forever—nor the hapless witnesses, for that matter. Miss Manners pictures them mesmerized by the promise of a denouement that never arrives. It is sure to interfere with their digestion.

For the sake of respect, your mother-in-law should be treated as if she were joking. Since your husband is sympathetic, he would be the ideal person to administer this treatment.

He could say, for example, **"Oh, Mom, I hate to tell you this, but I made up all those romances so you wouldn't think I was unpopular. The truth is, I never looked at a girl before Diana."** Or, **"Mother! When I stole Diana from convent school, I took an oath to preserve her innocence."**

A FALLBACK POSITION

DEAR MISS MANNERS—I am a married, 26-year-old career woman, and with every year that progresses, I seem to be asked more and more, *"When are you going to have a baby?"* I'm very tired of hearing this from co-workers and clients, as well as family and friends. Unfortunately, because of a medical condition, my husband and I are cautioned not to have a baby, although we would like one.

I've tried responses like **"How soon do you have to know?"** but it really doesn't seem to help. Would you please offer me an effective retort? I personally feel it's none of these people's business.

GENTLE READER—Actually, Miss Manners thought your answer was a scream, and she can't understand why it didn't work. What did these people possibly find to reply?

Oh, never mind. Those who cannot learn from a joke (this one being just this side of Miss Manners' line distinguishing jokes from insulting retorts, which she does not allow) must be told **"That is something I do not care to discuss."**

TEASING

DEAR MISS MANNERS—I wonder if you've come across this kind of "subtle" arrogance before: My husband's younger brother is a CEO who never leaves the office. Since he lives in the area of their father, he is the family will executor. Recently, he drew us a family tree, placing himself at the top and commenting, "and you are, well—you know, subordinates."

We said nothing, just smiled, but sometimes I think people should refrain from drawing trees that reveal what's between their ears.

GENTLE READER—Miss Manners is having trouble with your metaphor but not with your sentiment. The cure for arrogant relatives is gentle teasing. About the 43d time you address this brother as "Sir Treetop" he ought to crack.

TRAPPING

DEAR MISS MANNERS—A very wealthy and socially prominent local family, whom I shall call the Doozits, has a third-generation family business here, manufacturing and selling products internationally under the Doozit name.

My surname is also Doozit. Many times, people ask me, *"Are you related to THE Doozits?"* Usually, this appears to be inoffensive curiosity, but there have been occasions when I was snubbed when the questioner determined I am not related to the other Doozit family.

My usual answer is a simple "No," or perhaps a flippant, "No, but I wish I were!" But I feel a more assertive response is needed for the obvious snob ferreting out connections to the other Doozits.

GENTLE READER—All right, but Miss Manners trusts you to use this in a good-natured way, to tease your questioners rather than to denounce them.

The answer is **"THE Doozits? Why, yes, we are THE Doozits. Are there others? Oh, you mean the company. Why, no, we have nothing to do with that. Did they try to suggest that? Oh, dear. Sometimes people tend to** think they're related to us who are not, at least as far as we know."

A TIRESOME JOKE

DEAR MISS MANNERS—It has become something of a fad to tell "lawyer" jokes that imply that those of us in the profession are undesirable, unethical, some form of sub-human life or worse.

I can't help but take it personally when someone tells me one of these jokes because I, like my late father, am an attorney. What is the proper response to each when the person is a stranger, acquaintance, friend or relative?

GENTLE READER—You were wise to address your question to Miss Manners. There isn't another person in the society who would not use it as an opportunity to make another lawyer joke.

As you have found, you are not safe from relatives, friends, acquaintances or strangers. They all enjoy the new fun of insulting people to their faces (as opposed to the traditional method of behind their backs, which at least spared the victims the embarrassment of having to react).

The way to kill a joke is to treat it seriously. When you ask, solemnly, "Really? Have you had bad experiences with the law?" the offenders will, of course, come back with "Can't you take a joke?" To that bullying ploy, there is no more devastating response than **"Oh? Was that a joke?"**

MOCKERY

DEAR MISS MANNERS—Is there any appropriate reply to a person who is obviously mocking one's accent? Southern accents sound ignorant to Northern ears; Northern accents, in particular New York ones, sound rude and vulgar to Southern ears.

But what shall one do upon finding one's own regional accent made fun of to one's face by a stranger? For example, a group of professional women attending a conference inquired of another group, "Do y'all know where (a particular session is)?"

The reply, delivered in an exaggerated imitation of a Southern accent: "No, but we figger we'll be able to find it somehow." Does one merely have to accept this insult?

GENTLE READER—Bigoted remarks range from those that claim to be teasing to those that are frankly vicious, and they require different responses. This one being in the former category, you do not want to cut the perpetrators dead, only to have them follow you about, saying how they really envy you your adorable accent.

This does not mean that you have to accept the mocking. Rather, you must deny it the excuse of being a joke. The next time this happens, Miss Manners suggests you reply, with cool politeness, **"I beg your pardon, but I don't understand what you are saying."**

A prudent person will then drop the attempt at imitation and reply normally. A truly determined fool will continue by saying, perhaps even in the assumed accent, "I was just talking like you." The answer to that should, again, be, "I'm sorry, you'll have to speak more clearly." Eventually, even the biggest fool will notice that the joke is not working. It is even more embarrassing to claim that one was making a joke that bombed than to give up and agree that there was some sort of legitimate misunderstanding.

BIGOTED JOKES

DEAR MISS MANNERS—Is there a courteous way to express dissent/disapproval when one's guests or hosts make remarks or tell "jokes" that exhibit ugly prejudices? My impulse is to thrust my fork into the offender's ear, but I have managed to restrain myself.

I often host fairly large dinner parties for my husband's clients, and on occasion have been stunned to hear such remarks from seemingly educated, intelligent people at my table. But I've always believed guests must never be made to feel uncomfortable, and furthermore, it would be counterproductive to the purpose of the dinner to make an enemy of a client. I have also been at dinners where the host or hostess made similar remarks. As a guest, I hesitate to remonstrate.

When I am the hostess, I abruptly and rather pointedly change the subject. As a guest, I simply remain silent and decline any further invitations. When the remark is particularly offensive, I have, on occasion, raised my eyebrows and coldly (and falsely) informed the speaker that my mother was Jewish, black, Asian, lesbian, or whatever the target of the moment might be. This may strain credulity at times, but it does tend to silence the offending clod. Still, I am not satisfied with these responses.

GENTLE READER—Please allow Miss Manners to point out the hazards of pseudosocializing. One neither chooses one's business associates for the similarity of their private views nor feels as free to drop them when they prove seriously incompatible—two strong arguments for keeping job and social life separate.

That said, Miss Manners commends you on your techniques, all of which disassociate you from the bigotry without overt rudeness. If you wish to try another method, you might look at the offender wide-eyed and give an earnest explanation of the bigotry in question and of the kind of people who subscribe to it. There is nothing like the threat of a sociology lecture to encourage casual bigots to change the subject.

TIRED JOKES

DEAR MISS MANNERS—Is the "wry grimace" acceptable in social situations?

I have lived in Euless, Texas, for 14 years and I have yet to respond to questions about where I live without hearing, *"Oh, you live in Useless?"*

Humorous responses have lost their charm, and I hesitate to make a comment on the listener's acuity of hearing. Since silence leads to an awkward pause, I am considering the wry grimace, followed by a world-weary smile and the resumption of conversation on a different topic.

Am I being overly sensitive? Should I categorize trite humor with polite salutations—communication which lubricates the gears of social interaction, but without particular importance?

GENTLE READER—Miss Manners loves the Wry Grimace. Even after she found out it wasn't a cocktail.

You would now be justified in turning the expression on her. But you can depend on her never to make a pun or any other joke about the name of any person or hometown, or anyone's occupation or physical appearance. Automatic

Response Jokes tend to clog the gears of social interaction rather than lubricate them.

COMEDY ROUTINES

DEAR MISS MANNERS—I have two house rabbits as pets. They have the run of my home, are perfectly litter-box-trained as well as trained in general, and are wonderful, loving, intelligent pets whom I love very much.

Unfortunately, rabbit meat is a popular food staple around the world.

It both outrages and amazes me that many people—people who I would have considered friends—upon learning about my pet rabbits, make remarks along the lines of *"Aha, hasenpfeffer!"* or *"Is that what we're having for dinner?"* I get the feeling that these are attempts at comedy, but I do not take them that way.

How can I most tactfully handle the situation while serving notice that these remarks are unappreciated and hurtful?

GENTLE READER—The response that leaps to Miss Manners' mind is **"No, we're having the dog."**

After that, they are not likely to have the appetite to keep dishing out unpalatable comedy.

CHAPTER 9

THE APOLOGY AND OTHER FORMS OF DAMAGE CONTROL

ACCUSATORY REGRET

The two worst etiquette tasks are explaining and apologizing. These are so generally disliked that one of Miss Manners' contributions to the public happiness is decreeing that people who are behaving well need not make excuses for themselves. You can refuse an invitation or a proposal without having to produce convincing evidence that you are unable to comply—an expression of vague regret will do.

Yet Miss Manners finds that, in the very practice of courtesy, polite people seem to feel compelled to cast aspersions on innocent individuals and institutions. In the course of expressing courteous regret, an awful lot of ill-founded blame is tossed about with carefree unconcern for truth and reputations. Consider the usual conclusions to any apology that begins *"I tried to reach you, but—"*

"There must be something wrong with your answering machine."

"Didn't your roommate give you the message?"

"You know how the mails are these days."

"Didn't your child give you the message?"

"There must be something wrong with your fax machine."

"Didn't your secretary give you the message?"

"Didn't my secretary call you?"

Then there are the explanations for lateness, none of which seems to have involved a tardy start.

"The traffic was terrible."

"Your security system gave me a hard time."

"The bus broke down."

"Somebody gave me the wrong address."

"Six empty taxis passed me by."

"There must be some kind of a parade going through the city."

All this gets especially personal when an invitation is being refused, or an acceptance of one is being rescinded.

"My boss is making me stay late."

"I checked with Chris, who accepted an invitation for both of us and then forgot to tell me about it."

"My child doesn't want me to go."

"My parents came to visit unexpectedly."

Miss Manners' qualms about all this should not be understood as a cry for truth-in-explanations. Whatever offense is contained in these excuses is not as grievous as the unvarnished reality:

"You have a low priority in my thoughts, so I just never got around to it."

"I didn't want to stop what I was doing, and I figured it wouldn't be so bad to keep you waiting, as you probably have nothing special to do anyway."

"The last time I went to one of your parties, I promised myself I would never do it again, but then I got weak and said okay. Now I find I just can't face it."

No, Miss Manners only wants to limit the hurt being done to the reputations of the innocent. Thus, she offers a few simple rules about casting aspersions on unsullied parties who were minding their own business while you messed up your own arrangements.

Excuses that might actually hurt individuals—relatives or employees who might be reprimanded, or children who might be embarrassed—are banned.

However, others may agree to lend themselves in return for the same favor (**"I'd love to, but my boss keeps me on call"** in exchange for **"I'd love to, but my assistant tells me I can't make any more commitments"**). Parents are usually agreeable about being cited (**"I'd love to, but my mother won't let me"** or **"my father is so old-fashioned"**) on the grounds that nowadays a reputation for being strict, even if it is inaccurate, reflects credit on them.

The institutional excuse is more benign, although Miss Manners is beginning to feel that the post office and telephone companies have enough real troubles, and it isn't fair to make the excuse-receiver waste time calling his or her answering machine to find out if it really doesn't work.

The very safety and plausibility of these excuses has led to their overuse, to the extent of implausibility, which then hurts the recipient. No one believes that every single thank-you note you claim to have written in your life was lost in the mail.

The best excuse is therefore **"I must have been out of my mind when I—"** forgot to call, misjudged the time or accepted an invitation for a day I'd scheduled something else. The blameless person always seeks to blame him or herself.

UNENDING REGRET

DEAR MISS MANNERS—I was boarding an airport shuttle and was holding an un-lidded (stupid me!) cup of hot coffee. Quarters were close, and I was klutzy and I spilled some coffee on a fellow traveler's down coat. I immediately dropped my luggage, grabbed some paper towels, offered to go for water or soap, and apologized. I gave her my name and address and begged her to have her coat cleaned and to send me the bill.

The victim of my stupidity said nothing and scrubbed away at her coat. I feel as though I embarrassed the poor woman by drawing attention to her, and I can't make reparations for that as easily as I can for the coat. Since she said not a word during the entire exchange, I can't really gauge the degree of her anger or her forgiveness. Did I do the right thing?

GENTLE READER—Much as she would like to relieve you, Miss Manners cannot say that spilling coffee on someone is the right thing to do. But even etiquette recognizes that accidents happen, and your second act, that of spilling apologies and offers of restitution all over the place, was right.

Actually, we seem to be talking about your second through 88th acts, and perhaps now is the time to stop. One should always apologize until the victim finally says **"Oh, that's quite all right; don't worry about it,"** but yours does not seem to have been polite enough to manage this. It is therefore she, not you, who should be feeling pangs now.

UNACCEPTED REGRET

DEAR MISS MANNERS—I embarrassed myself deeply this evening.

I worked late, then had to go to the grocery store, tired and irritable. At the store's vestibule, a mother was calling to her five-year-old through the "in" door to get off the mat so the door would open. I instantly created an image of a child staying on the mat to annoy mommy (just as some jokesters hold revolving doors still) and I stepped forward and yelled, "Move it" through the door in a fit of impatient anger.

Actually I think the child was trying to get a cart and didn't realize she was on the mat. Luckily, she did not seem to realize whom I was yelling at. But her mother did and was shocked—as was I. I immediately apologized as profusely as I could, trying not to offer excuses or call my behavior anything but rude. She remained shocked, and did not respond; I remained embarrassed, shopped quickly, and fled the store.

I would have felt better had my apology been accepted in some way, but I suppose that is too much to ask under the circumstances. Once I had lost my temper, was there anything more I could have done? I am generally a polite, considerate person, which makes an episode like this especially disturbing. I don't like to fail my ideals in such an ugly way.

GENTLE READER—Miss Manners commends you for your ideals and for your embarrassment and apologies in connection with this lapse. Under the circumstances, all you could do was to apologize.

It would have been nice if the mother could have accepted your apology more graciously, but you might bear in mind that she could be suffering from the same tiredness that dimmed your own manners.

The discomfort you feel is there to remind you to be wary of the danger of expressing irritability to innocent people. Miss Manners promises you that it will fade—leaving, she hopes, its lesson.

THE DOUBLE APOLOGY

DEAR MISS MANNERS—My husband is about to retire. I made the mistake of telling him one morning, when he left food, garbage, etc., all over the kitchen, "You messy man, clean up behind you!" The result is that he now leaves things everywhere around the house. Never cares for clothing or anything he touches.

How, if possible, do I correct this terrible mistake? He will soon be home with me all day.

GENTLE READER—Well, now, you were rude (or so Miss Manners gathers, in spite of the cute phrasing) and he is retaliating by being spiteful. We can't have the two of you spending all day together like that, can we?

Miss Manners recommends a quaint old custom called the apology. A functioning household apology is kindly said, does not address the question of who was more at fault and is not an opportunity to restate the original complaint.

Thus, *"I shouldn't have snapped at you, but I can't stand your being such a pig, and now you're being spiteful"* is not what Miss Manners has in mind. But **"I'm sorry I was after you about being messy"** is a clear cue to reply **"Well, I'm sorry I was messy."**

At least two days should pass between this exchange and an unrelated conversation that opens with a pleasant "Well, dear, now that you're going to be home more, perhaps we should talk about how to divide up the household chores."

BEYOND APOLOGY

DEAR MISS MANNERS—I planted my foot firmly and deeply in my mouth. Short of using a crowbar, which would result in serious damage to my teeth, what can I do to fix this situation?

My wife and I were watching my daughter's soccer game when a mother right next to us asked, "Why is it that the coach's kid gets all the free kicks?"

"Because he's the most obnoxious kid on the team," I answered, softly enough so my voice would not carry to anyone other than my wife and that woman. "Don't you come to the practices?"

Almost as soon as I opened my mouth, my wife tried to deliver the equivalent of a kick to the shins under the table, but lacking a table, she made her actions too subtle for me to recognize. (Okay, you may be right in your wicked thought that it was not that her actions were too subtle, but that their target was—is—too dense.)

By now, you have guessed that I was unwittingly (and dimwittingly) speaking to the coach's wife. I must say that I feel I was set up, but that is neither here nor there. Neither is my belief (and my wife's) that the statement was correct.

I know that I should probably refrain from answering rhetorical questions, and be able, at least, to identify any person I am addressing. But is there any way to retrieve the situation, even partly?

An apology is in order, but that would make clear that I was not speaking in jest. I am not concerned that my daughter will suffer repercussions, but I wish to do what is right, if only (and that is not to say merely) with regard to etiquette.

GENTLE READER—Miss Manners doesn't know why she feels sorry for you—you should never make such a remark, especially as it is about a child, to anyone, except the wife of your bosom in the privacy of your home—but she does. It just goes to show what a little groveling will do.

Yet she agrees with you that an apology in this case would erase the only possible feeble out you have available. If your wife, who sounds like a good sort, is willing to bail you out, Miss Manners suggests that she say to the lady in question: **"You know, there's something that worries me. My husband says he is sure you knew he was spinning out your little joke about your child the other day, but I'm not so sure. It didn't come out funny, the way it was intended."**

BEYOND ACCEPTANCE

DEAR MISS MANNERS—I overheard a very insulting remark made by a colleague. The person later apologized. However, the remark he made was essentially irreversible, and I refused to accept his apology. I then became the villain, not he. Is there a rule in social etiquette that one must accept an apology, no matter how obnoxious the insult?

GENTLE READER—This depends on how quick a talker the insulter is. If he or she can present a plausible tale of not having meant the remark to be an insult, the apology must be accepted.

Jokes, teasings, misunderstandings and claiming to have oneself the quality for which you were insulted are the standard excuses. Granted that these may not be true, Miss Manners wishes to point out that your position of overhearing the remark leaves you vulnerable to charges of not having heard it absolutely correctly.

But yes, she reluctantly acknowledges that there are, in extreme cases, permanent insults that justify ceasing to acknowledge that the insulter exists. In that case, the matter ought to be clear enough for others to understand that the villain was the insulter, not the victim.

SEEKING RECONCILIATION

DEAR MISS MANNERS—I coordinated a farewell luncheon with a co-worker for another co-worker she is very close with. To help her, because she was busy with a lot of work, I collected the money, purchased the gift, and assisted in organizing the luncheon.

She did not show any appreciation for this help, and when I asked, she became angry and stated that she was stressed out and did not want to express appreciation. All I wanted to hear was, "Thank you. I appreciate what you have done."

The final straw came when I did not attend a birthday luncheon for another co-worker because I was upset that she did not show the slightest appreciation. Since then, she has not spoken to me. What did I do wrong? Did I overreact to her sensitivity? What can I do to resume the friendship?

GENTLE READER—Friendship? What friendship? It seems to Miss Manners that what you have is an etiquette stand-off.

It is, of course, rude not to express thanks for a favor. It is also rude to request thanks for a favor one has done, rude to air a grievance by boycotting an event involving a third party and rude to air a grievance by refusing to speak to someone.

You can point out that the first lapse was hers, with the others following from it. She might make the case that office parties are not her responsibility alone, so that you were doing no more than your duty. So, since you ask, yes, everybody is wrong and overreacting (except Miss Manners for going to pieces over the claim that being either stressed or ignored justifies a rude retaliation).

Blessedly, that is not your only question. Miss Manners admires you for that final question of what you can do to make things right. The answer is: Do not attempt to sort through the rights and wrongs. Simply say something nice and friendly, as if nothing had ever happened, and, if your colleague brings up the past, offer your own apology without asking for hers, and drop it. If more people were concerned with being reconciled than right, the world would be a better place.

CHAPTER 10

COVERING FOR OTHERS

THE ELDERLY

"Eccentric" is the polite term for the irascible elderly, and "respectfully" the polite way to treat such people. Etiquette is succinct and firm on that issue: Respect is owed to age, regardless of any deficiency of personal merit on the part of the aged one.

What if an old person is more appropriately described as impossible, and regularly engages in wildly provocative behavior? Suppose that respect-worthy old person makes insulting and baseless accusations to relatives or friends? Or yells at strangers? Or outspokenly expresses bigotry? Or answers kind deeds with indifference or hostility? Or threatens nonsensical but nevertheless troublesome lawsuits?

Miss Manners hardly knows of a more difficult test of etiquette than applying the rule of respect for age to those whom age has cruelly robbed of similar attributes of civilization.

Because this impairment is a comparatively rare occurrence among the elderly, etiquette does not provide rules for dealing with those who no longer have manners, as it does for children who do not yet have them. The rude child is no treasure, and probably nobody can bear him but his parents, who may be having a hard time too. But small children are generally accorded some leniency for "not knowing any better," while people who used to know better are not.

Miss Manners is not suggesting that there is an answer as simple as laughing off damaging behavior. A variety of tactics, nearly all of them difficult, must be employed in such situations to maintain everyone's dignity, not least being that of the victim of uncontrolled words and actions.

She does begin by saying that society in general should be aware of the possibility of such a problem, instead of assuming that all offensive acts are reasoned. One should be prepared to bring both surface skepticism and deeper understanding to any uncharacteristically outrageous behavior. Strangers or acquaintances should be able to let such acts pass without disparagement.

Anyone close to a person with such a problem is going to spend a lot of time apologizing. Complaints against others on the part of an extremely difficult person have to be investigated, but at the same time, tremendous tact must be exercised to avoid insulting the perhaps randomly accused. The key phrases are **"He doesn't really mean it," "Please understand that she is not herself," "I hope you'll remember that he loves you dearly, and was always happy to see you before this came on him"** and **"It's not that you did anything—it's just the way she is now."**

Miss Manners does not consider this an indignity to the subject. It is the greatest respect to assume that one would want done, on one's behalf, whatever is necessary to avoid hurting others.

It behooves those who are the targets to accept such apologies gracefully. In some cases, the compassionate person who has inadvertently set off hostile behavior has no choice but to cut off the ruined relationship and try to preserve unsullied memories.

If the problem is directed toward a caretaker, as sometimes tragically happens, that may not be humanely possible. Not reacting to provocation is difficult enough in ordinary relationships; doing so when one is badly treated by someone whom one is sacrificing to help is good exercise for sainthood. There is a strong and understandable craving for cooperation and gratitude when one is doing a difficult job.

The apologies made to oneself—**"I know she doesn't mean it, I know she doesn't mean it," "It's not really he speaking"**—are the hardest to accept.

THE INDISCREET

DEAR MISS MANNERS—Mrs. C., who is one of my best friends on the earth, was hostess at an informal dinner when a somewhat awkward social situation ensued, placing unfamiliar guests, my date and myself in an uncomfortable position.

A bit of background: A few years ago, Mrs. C. and I were involved in a romantic relationship that failed, but left us very good friends. Recently, she married, and her new husband has become a fairly good acquaintance of mine. This is a happy situation that is often desired but not always obtainable. The young woman I was escorting to this party knows the situation and thinks of it in a like manner. There were a number of guests who knew nothing of this past history.

Mrs. C. and I were swapping amusing tales of past misadventures, giving no indication of our past intimacies. We were all laughing over one story when a young female guest asked how we knew each other. The highly amusing story of how we met through a club was what some of the "informed" people expected. To the dismay of many, Mrs. C. blurted out in a short fashion, *"We were lovers."*

I felt like crawling away, hopefully unnoticed. There was an uncomfortable silence that followed, and several guests proceeded to stare at my date. Both of us were sharing an undesired spotlight. The statement was wrong for Mrs. C. to make, but I am asking how to handle it.

GENTLE READER—Wrong? It is an etiquette nightmare.

If Mrs. C. does not understand the basic rule governing past intimacies—that all secrets are joint property, to be released only with the consent of both parties—surely the rule against embarrassing one's guests should have stopped her. She sacrificed your feelings, those of the lady with you and probably those of other guests. (That every party contains some people who consider their evening made by such goings on does not lessen her guilt.)

Mrs. C.'s apologizing and swearing never to do it again should be a condition of your continuing friendship. In fact, the apology called for needs to be in the highest (or one might say the lowest) category—groveling. She should claim to have been temporarily out of her mind, as a result of anxiety over whether the salad leaves had wilted.

As for handling such a surprise burst of indiscretion, Miss Manners suggests some smoothly ambiguous statement, such as **"Oh, for heaven's sake, darling, people will take you seriously."** (The "darling" is in there because there is hardly a better confirmation than petulant denial.)

Should Mrs. C. not take the clue to back down, but recklessly persist by saying *"I was serious,"* you would be justified in replying gently, **"Really? I had no idea"** before suggesting that the company may wish to talk about something else.

THE MALEVOLENT

DEAR MISS MANNERS—My mother perceives events inaccurately and she has a weakness for embellishment. When she recounts an incident, she utters a semblance of truth but puts a malevolent spin on it.

Because of her sweet-sounding voice, she can portray herself as a hapless victim of other people's bullying and she can work up sympathetic listeners into quite a rage in her behalf. Most people cannot believe my mother would do anything devious but she has created tremendous havoc.

Is there a discreet way to warn people about her manipulations without badmouthing her or appearing to be a backstabber? I often keep quiet because saying anything remotely critical of her casts suspicion on me. But it's difficult to silently watch her create discord between two people, or set up somebody for embarrassment.

GENTLE READER—Miss Manners is not generally in favor of hinting that one's relatives are malevolent troublemakers either, but in the interests of preventing the sweet lady from sowing discord, she might make an exception.

As you realize, the challenge here is to undercut your mother without withholding the respect to which she is entitled. Not easy. You cannot contradict your mother, either to her face or behind her back. But you can help interpret what she means, a family duty. Therefore, you can say **"Oh, Mother, you don't mean that the way it sounds,"** or **"Mother's a marvelous storyteller, but she likes to dramatize. She'd be horrified if she thought it came out as if she thought those people were being mean."**

THE MUDDLED

DEAR MISS MANNERS—At a long meeting, my boss twice referred to a business associate, with whom we were engaging in a joint venture, by the wrong name. Our associate did not correct him, but seemed perplexed at the error.

I considered doing nothing and leaving it to the two of them to work out. I considered passing my boss a note, but that would have been rather obvious under the circumstances. I chose, instead, to take the next opportunity to address our associate by his correct name.

Although my boss began to use the proper name, later apologized for his error and did not seem to be angry with me, I am still wondering if I took the correct action—if, indeed, any action was appropriate. No doubt, Miss Manners would have been more sure of herself.

GENTLE READER—Well, yes, Miss Manners is nothing if not sure of herself. She would have done exactly what you did, except that she would have omitted worrying about it.

It is a kindness to stop someone from repeating an error (not to mention wisdom to rescue a boss from looking bad), but essential that this be done discreetly. As the idea is to save embarrassment, it should not be done by causing more.

THE GROSS

DEAR MISS MANNERS—What should be my reaction when someone close to me accidentally spits a small piece of food out of their mouth, which lands on me? In contrast, what should be my reaction if I am the guilty party?

This happened at a $50 a plate banquet. A woman to my

right, a good friend, unknowingly spit out a piece of food which landed on my suit coat. I just ignored it and tried to engage people in conversation to my left. It eventually fell off when I got up.

GENTLE READER—Every once in a while, someone comes up with a perfectly legitimate etiquette problem that is nevertheless so gross that the only way to deal with it is to pretend that it never happened. Congratulations on today's submission.

Congratulations, also, on the way you handled it. The only addition Miss Manners would suggest would be a napkin. You could have removed the item inconspicuously— well, comparatively inconspicuously—by absentmindedly dabbing at the situation with your napkin, while firmly maintaining a line of unrelated conversation with the guilty party.

The hapless soul who commits the error can only hope that a fire will break out in another part of the room, during which a quick dab to remove the evidence will pass unnoticed.

CHAPTER 11

AT A LOSS FOR WORDS

UNSPEAKABLE ANNOUNCEMENTS

Miss Manners has enormous sympathy with people who don't know what to say in response to their acquaintances' announcements because of the nature of what those acquaintances are announcing:

"We just called to tell you that we're breaking up. We thought you'd like to hear it from both of us together."

"I'm going to have my breasts done."

"We have a great new system for beating the tax law."

"I now realize I never should have had children."

"We're going on vacation that week, because our doctor told us that's the prime time for us to conceive."

"We're going to get married as soon as he tells his wife."

"We're not getting married because then her ex-husband's payments would stop."

"Our son is finally going into drug rehabilitation."

"Our daughter is suing her boyfriend for child support."

"My sister's having an abortion."

"I've found God."

"I have a new lover."

"My hard disk crashed."

That last one is easy. Profound condolences are required. Otherwise, etiquette has not come to terms with the modern habit of turning what used to be confidences into general announcements.

Poured into the ears of carefully chosen intimate friends, such information may have the desired effect. Aimed scattershot, these declarations are bound to reach some people who not only have no particular sympathy with the person making the announcement—which polite people take care to disguise, there being no limit on the number of good wishes we can each dispense—but who disagree with the very premise on which sympathetic understanding is expected.

If Miss Manners wants to enjoin them from responding to an announcement, even an injudicious one, with a lecture—and she does, she does—she ought to be able to offer a noncommittal yet polite response. Unfortunately, the reasonable response—*"Why are you telling me this?"*—is not polite. And the polite responses don't always seem reasonable.

Do you congratulate someone on the prospect of a new bosom, wait until the result is unveiled, so to speak, or offer condolences on the need? When a person announces success in breaking the law, are congratulations in order? Should those who are caught be offered condolences? Or should a law-abiding citizen offer these the other way around?

Miss Manners would dearly love to solve the etiquette aspect by throwing away all those additional milestones. There is a great deal being announced that the public at large doesn't need to know. The efficiency and fun of hearing gossip firsthand, rather than having to wait until it is whispered behind the back of the person concerned, is not worth the awkwardness of having to respond.

In the meantime, Miss Manners is making do by frantically wishing everyone the best at all times. She also recommends **"How nice *for* you"** aimed at anyone who isn't actually in tears when making the announcement, and **"Oh, dear,"** for anyone who is.

ISSUING ADVISORIES

DEAR MISS MANNERS—When does one tell another individual that one has AIDS?

Although I can no longer work, I am not an invalid. I frequently go out to social events and quasi-social events (my sister, with whom I live, is a physician and frequently required to go to those events you describe as business masquerading as social). I also go out to the local bar frequently in the evening.

To anyone who did not know me, I appear perfectly healthy, and many times I am. I do not go out when obviously ill, but I have a sliding scale as far as fevers are concerned: anything under 100.5 and I can go out. I do not want to give up a social life—I enjoy people immensely, enjoy meeting new people, and am doing my best to live life to the fullest extent I can manage.

I would ordinarily say it is none of their business, and as far as health is concerned, it is I who am running the risk of getting ill from being out. Many people do know that I have AIDS, and others whom I meet are likely to find out. I am 37 and good-looking enough to have people attempt to pick me up.

Some people get very upset at shaking my hand, sitting next to me in a bar, or using the facilities after me. If I in some way forewarn them, I can usually set their minds at ease, or at least allow them to break off conversation and move on to someone else.

Friends have pointed out that I frequently introduce

myself with some version of *"Hi, I'm Tom, I have AIDS."* On the other hand, if I neglect to slip it into the conversation somewhere and they find out later, two common reactions are that I am trying to present myself under false pretenses, possibly endangering their health or their peace of mind, or that they begin circulating through the party or whatever warning people that I am a positive menace.

Neither is conducive to my peace of mind (which is more important now that I have mild episodic dementia, and stress can adversely affect my health, landing me in bed with something more life-threatening) or to the social standing of my sister and my friends.

Often after I have told someone, they immediately confess their ignorance and curiosity and I have an excellent topic to begin conversation, while enlightening the other person. I have made some excellent friends in this manner, and have even had gracious thank you's with follow-up invitations for lunch or some other event.

How do I tell people? What do I tell them? When do I tell them? The blunt way seems to work in general, but it may also be rude. I want others to feel comfortable meeting me, although I know not everyone is capable or willing to do that. Still, I would like to give them the option before either of us becomes embarrassed or ill at ease.

GENTLE READER—It is important to distinguish here between issuing a warning and offering a confidence. The first is morally obligatory, to anyone likely to be medically affected; the second is voluntary, toward anyone whose reaction you guess will make it worthwhile to you.

Miss Manners need hardly mention that the former category consists of those whom you delicately describe as attempting to pick you up. It is, potentially, their "business."

Toward people with whom you might do less intensive socializing that will not put them at risk, you need not feel obliged to give your confidence, even if they are likely to find out later. It is not their business.

However, you say you want to talk about your AIDS, for social, educational and conversational reasons. And you are prepared to take the chance that the announcement will be greeted unsympathetically.

So the question becomes how you tell people without unduly startling them. Miss Manners suggests that you would find it useful to go over your dialogue substituting say, cancer, a disease that was once, but is no longer, ridiculously considered to carry a stigma.

Suppose someone you just met at a party said, in effect, *"Hi! I'm Andrew and I have cancer!"*

However kindly a human being you might be, surely you would think, if not say, "Well, what do you expect me to do about it?" There is something about such a bald confidence from a stranger that precludes the natural development of sympathies that even a momentary acquaintance would produce.

Preliminary conversation, when two people are attempting to get to know each other, properly consists of vague questioning (as opposed to full-blast investigative techniques, now common but nevertheless rude). There is the chance for you to say **"Actually, I'm an engineer, but I'm retired now because of my AIDS,"** or **"One of my chief interests is AIDS education, since I'm a victim of AIDS myself."** This gives the other person a chance to take up the topic, or to excuse himself.

POSTPONING CONFRONTATION

DEAR MISS MANNERS—I was taught it is very rude to criticize other people in public. My husband does criticize me, and even yells at me in public, which I find humiliating. I have told him (privately) not to, but he continues to bother me in this fashion.

What I want to know is, what should I do in these situations? Should I ignore him or what? I do not want to create a scene.

GENTLE READER—In answering your question by suggesting a dignified way to cope with this problem, Miss Manners wants to make it clear that she does not believe a husband's deliberate humiliation of a wife, after such warnings, can be dealt with as a surface problem. This is not what Miss Manners would classify as merely an unfortunate etiquette transgression on the part of an otherwise well-meaning person.

The answer is a calm, cool, **"Yes, dear, whatever you say, we'll discuss it later."** This registers the idea that you are not acquiescing to him, but have simply decided to avoid a public scene.

WHEN THINGS ARE NOT OKAY

Someone was reporting a highway shooting that seemed, and indeed proved, to be fatal. The caller asked for an ambulance, while stating her fear that her husband was dying.

"Okay," replied the emergency operator.

The caller repeated her request, adding, "He's dying, he's really dying."

"All right," said the operator.

"Please hurry."

"Okay," the transcript shows that the operator repeated. "We've got them en route."

The caller then described the victim's bloody state and her belief that he was dying.

There was another *"okay,"* followed by the repeated assurance that the ambulance was en route.

"Please," repeated the caller.

"Okay."

In such a tragic emergency, one would not think the details to be of much account. But Miss Manners finds herself struck by the repeated use of the word "okay" and its equivalent, "all right."

Obviously, this was intended to mean "Yes, I have understood what you are telling me, and I am sending the help you need." Time and clarity being essential, "okay" is a word that is quickly understood.

Even Miss Manners would not want an emergency operator to take the precious time to indulge in expressions of alarm or sympathy. Crisp efficiency is what is needed. But "okay" does not strike her as the way to convey this. It strikes her as a way to plant the idea, as erroneous as that may be, that the call is not being taken seriously.

"Okay" is a word that is commonly used to express casual approbation—"fine with me." Sometimes it can convey a mild lack of interest—a kind of low-key "So what?" Or that what is being deemed okay is normal and not unexpected. It can also be understood to substitute for an even more unfortunate response, which had a vogue that Miss Manners hopes is mercifully over: *"I hear what you're saying."* What that meant was "I have to listen to you, but don't think for a minute that this means I agree with you."

Miss Manners does not imagine that any such callous meanings are intended when people who are taking reports—emergencies or simple complaints—use "okay" as their standard response. But she considers it an unfortunate choice of words that can add to the caller's sense of devastation. Obviously, everything is not okay. Apparently, to be told that it is can be frustrating and infuriating.

In less crucial instances, for example, one calls to report that a mistake was made by a business or service: "You sent me the wrong item," or "You came and fixed my appliance, but it still doesn't work right."

"*Okay,*" says the person who took the complaint.

"What do you mean, 'okay'?" the complainer thinks if not actually asks. "It's not okay! I'm calling to tell you that things are not okay! Understand?"

"*Okay.*"

And while the caller in a truly serious emergency may hardly notice the details of what is said, Miss Manners cannot help but think this person too might feel an additional worry from being told that the situation is okay.

Emergency operators would be well instructed to confirm the essential information instead by repeating it. A repetition of the address of the disaster would be a more useful response than that sloppy affirmation.

In nonemergencies, there is time for acknowledging that something wrong has happened. There, a brief expression of sympathy with the caller's predicament, accompanied by a promise to attend to the matter, can do wonders to defuse anger. Miss Manners is not convinced by the argument that an immediate, calming, polite **"I'm sorry,"** in response to such a complaint, is a premature acknowledgment of guilt that would throw the lawsuit that the furious customer is bound to bring. "I'm sorry" can be interpreted to mean sorrow that the situation exists, no matter whose fault it is. Besides, the likelihood of the customer's sustaining enough anger to sue dramatically diminishes in the face of regret and sympathy, which are attitudes that few people, however provoked, can resist.

GRACE UNDER PRESSURE

DEAR MISS MANNERS—What standard of behavior is required of a lady during labor and delivery?

Having previously gone through unmedicated childbirth, I know that there are times when one feels testy, and that these are exactly the times that nurses and so forth ask questions and give instructions that have to be dealt with.

If one gets a bit short-tempered, should she apologize later, even though she may not know exactly whom she was cross with or how badly she behaved? Does one apologize for being noisy, if one has managed to remain cooperative? If so, to whom?

GENTLE READER—Miss Manners' appreciation of this question—that a lady who is under such trying circumstances should worry about the feelings of others—does not prompt her to dismiss it. She is not of the school that believes that pain automatically cancels all etiquette requirements.

Noise is rather an expected part of the procedure and not objectionable in itself. But if "short-tempered" means attempting to alleviate one's discomfort by accusations and outbursts against others, apologies are certainly in order. Nurses and other hospital employees may have a professional understanding of such behavior without being totally immune to its human consequences.

In any case, you should be thanking them for their

assistance. A lack of knowledge as to whether you behaved badly can gracefully be covered by adding **"I hope I didn't cause you too much trouble."**

PASSING

DEAR MISS MANNERS—When I was a child, I had the misfortune to be molested by a man my family trusted. I kept silent, but I never forgot what happened. Fortunately, I don't have to worry that my silence is enabling him to use another child in the despicable manner in which he used me, because he died many years ago.

The problem is that we still have social contact with his widow and their adult offspring. At a gathering a few weeks ago, everyone was reminiscing about what a fine man the deceased had been. I felt uncomfortable, but I certainly couldn't tell the awful truth to the innocent relatives, so I remained silent. I am relieved that my silence went unremarked.

But what if I am not so lucky another time? What would be a good response if asked why I am not joining in singing his praises? The only one I can think of is, "Oh, I'm afraid I couldn't possibly do him justice."

GENTLE READER—Clever, but Miss Manners doesn't know that she would go that far. While admiring your kindness in not unnecessarily disillusioning the survivors, she is not sure she would be so generous as to leave open the possibility that you might have been awed by his greatness. You run the risk of their pleading to hear more.

A total pass would be **"I'm sure you miss him."** Perhaps slightly more satisfying to you would be **"Oh, I'm not going to say anything—I was only a child."**

A STARTLING DISCOVERY

DEAR MISS MANNERS—I recently discovered that I have a 15-year-old son from a very brief (dare I say) relationship. The week of that (relationship), I met a young lady who would soon become my wife, and from that union, two sons have resulted.

When I introduce this young man to friends and acquaintances, they all seem to be at a loss for words, or make stupid comments like "Oh, I didn't know you had three sons," "Where did the third one come from?" or "Oh, I see you have three sons now; what's going on?"

I would like to be able to stop any unnecessary, ignorant questions that may hurt and embarrass my son or myself. I am almost getting afraid to tell people who he is for fear of what the next humiliating question may be. What is the proper way to introduce my "new" son? Might I say, **"This is my son from a previous relationship"**?

GENTLE READER—Yes, why not? Miss Manners yields to no one in her distaste for nosiness, and she agrees that grilling people on personal matters is not to be tolerated. But even she allows that when one has a friend with two teenaged sons and he suddenly has three teenaged sons, it is reasonable to check to see if one had miscounted.

So your situation requires a bit of explanation. Not much, just a bit. Say something between the cabbage patch and the vivid picture you gave Miss Manners of what must have been an extremely eventful week in your life.

Offering such an explanation before you are asked will discourage the polite from pursuing the matter, mesmerized with curiosity though they may be. It will not stop the determinedly rude, as we all know. They will have to be told firmly that your delight in your future with your son is what now interests you, not raking up the past.

FORGETFULNESS

It doesn't seem right that one of the greatest social crimes is committed by those who are innocent of malicious intent. Surely, meaning well should count in etiquette, of all fields.

But not in the case of this crime, which is—

It is—

It—

Yes.

Well.

It's— whatever.

Please forgive Miss Manners. Her memory isn't what it never was.

Oh, yes. The crime is forgetfulness.

Forgetfulness, the most understandable of slips, can also unfortunately be the most unforgivable.

Forgetting the name of an acquaintance is taken as a horrendous insult. Forgetting how to spell or pronounce such a name is hardly any better. Forgetting which of the many choices of separate or melded surnames and honorifics a couple prefers is tantamount to declaring war on their personal philosophy.

Forgetting an occasion, such as a birthday, is taken as a symbolic dismissal of enough vile significance to plunge the celebrant who had expected to be remembered into a murky mixture of despair and resentment.

Forgetting a social engagement is inevitably perceived as a snub so callous as to constitute an excuse for ending a friendship.

And forgetting that one has already told someone the

same story or made the same confidence (complete with "You're the only person I'm telling . . .") is taken as a sign that it is time for the speaker to retire from the social scene altogether.

What, then, is someone with a faulty memory supposed to do?

Miss Manners does not provide exercises for improving the memory. Her responsibility should be to provide methods of covering up a lapse of memory, or making amends for it. But the truth is that the available methods are pretty lame. And potentially dangerous. There is no use saying that honesty is the best policy to someone who has charmingly admitted "I know I know you, but I just can't quite place you" if the reply is "I was your first husband." And such coy tricks as "How do you spell that?" fail when the answer is "J-O-N-E-S."

All Miss Manners can suggest is total self-abasement: **"I must be losing my mind. I know your name as well as I know my own. I'll never forgive myself. Never. I don't deserve to be your friend . . . ,"** etc. The idea is to so wear out the offended person that it becomes easier to forgive than to listen to more of the same.

Forgetting occasions and social events is expensive as well as taxing. One must send a present or flowers along with self-incrimination. Miss Manners' best advice is to fortify oneself in advance with both vigilance and humility.

Advance vigilance consists of checking the spelling of names, keeping lists of people's family members and hanging the calendar of birthdays and social events where one can't help seeing it—over the bed in poster-sized type, for example. Advance humility means refraining from thinking, let alone making, accusations. *"I'm sure you never told me"* and *"Who stole my keys?"* are expressions that should be forgotten forever.

Miss Manners also recommends tolerance on the part of those who are never forgetful—or who don't remember when they have been. The polite person doesn't wait to be remembered or not, but announces his or her own name at every opportunity.

It is not only because one may soon become forgetful oneself that one should cherish the forgetful. It should be remembered that the forgetful can be wonderful friends: They forget the incident when you made a fool of yourself. They forget any little slights and grudges, which may be less noble than forgiving but is easier and more effective. They don't say "I told you so" when you get into trouble, because they forget if they actually did. And they forget that the person you now say you love is the one you once said was a monster.

Did Miss Manners already tell you that?

MAKING ACCUSATIONS

DEAR MISS MANNERS—Is there any polite way to phrase an accusation against someone you suspect is guilty of an annoying petty theft?

A short time ago, I boarded an airplane transportation bus at my hotel. Upon arrival at the airport, I debarked. Immediately, I realized I had left my expensive pair of sunglasses on the seat beside me, but I stepped aside to allow the other passengers to alight and pick up their luggage. Alas, when I returned to my seat, I discovered the glasses had vanished.

As I claimed my bag, I was tempted to say, "I'd appreciate

it if the person who picked up my glasses would return them to me," but that seemed to have an accusing tone I didn't intend, since I wasn't sure to whom it should be directed.

I never did say anything, but I continue to have the nagging thought that there must have been some polite way I could have managed to entice the glasses back into my possession, or at least have conveyed my outrage so that I could assure myself that the glasses would only be worn in the future with some degree of discomfort.

Would Miss Manners have kept her silence in the situation, as I finally did, or would she have devised some diplomatic way of asking for their return?

GENTLE READER—The glasses were on the sofa in the hotel lobby, where you collected your baggage while waiting for the bus. Miss Manners didn't exactly see them there, but that is probably because you stole her lorgnette.

Perhaps you do not care for this tone. Miss Manners doesn't either. She finds it exceedingly unpleasant that having yourself been guilty of carelessness, you are ready to accuse others of being criminally responsible for your loss.

It is not just a question of addressing the innocent along with the guilty, but of taking it for granted that someone besides yourself was guilty.

What Miss Manners would have done, out of humility as well as politeness, would be to inquire piteously whether any of her fellow passengers would be kind enough to help her look for her glasses. Then you could have the grace to be apologetic when someone picked them up from where you had knocked them off the seat. Even such a rogue as you suppose to have taken advantage of you could have then produced the glasses and returned them to you.

DEALING WITH A NUISANCE

DEAR MISS MANNERS—On a flight from Sacramento to Dallas, a child kicked the back of my seat for over three hours, keeping me awake and irritated. The mother kept telling me, "I'mmmm soooory" the entire time. I am determined not to let a future juvenile delinquent and child-parent do this to me again. What is the best way to deal with this?

GENTLE READER—You might offer to exchange seats with the mother. Miss Manners realizes that would put you next to the offending child, but imagines that if you say, sweetly, **"I imagine you're used to this, but I'm not,"** she will decline the offer and deal with the child. The alternative is to ask the flight attendant quietly to have the child put off the airplane.

THE MISSED SIGNAL

DEAR MISS MANNERS—Several times recently, I have been asked personal grooming questions, or family-oriented questions, in a very public setting, by persons who are mildly retarded and are working in service positions. There have been others present, and going into detail would not be correct and would only serve to encourage this behavior.

Miss Manners must realize that I do understand that they have meant no harm. But the thought of discussing my hair coloring or whether a young lady who is pregnant is married or not, while waiting to be seated in a restaurant, being offered canapés, or being served has truly not only put me off, but made me very uncomfortable.

I have tried to give a simple, one-line response, such as

"Thank you for the compliment" or "The baby is due in June," accompanied by a genuine smile. For most people, that would seem to be enough.

But I have noticed that it is not only rude, but impossible to ignore persistent questioning from persons who are almost childlike in their innocence.

GENTLE READER—Etiquette does consider motivation, so Miss Manners agrees that you are quite right not to put these questions in the same category as those from snoops who have merely decided to ignore the social barriers of which they are well aware.

In fact, there are so many of the latter around, that anyone with the least innocence left could easily get the mistaken notion that such questions were welcome.

But while etiquette requires you to be polite, it does not require you to violate your privacy. If the social signals sent by your evasive answers are not caught, you must politely but firmly explain **"This is not something I will discuss."** Persistence, such as the further question "Why not?," must be answered with a polite **"I won't discuss that either."**

THE MISSING HUSBAND

DEAR MISS MANNERS—After several months of courtship, my boyfriend and I, both in our early 30's and well established in professional careers, experienced a birth control failure and I became pregnant. We do not live together.

In our pre-intimacy conversations, we both expressed a desire to have a committed relationship and "settle down." Also, at that time, I let him know that if a pregnancy occurred, I would not seek an abortion.

Upon learning of the pregnancy, his response was that he was not ready for marriage or a child. Now that I am in my third month, he is all but completely absent from my life. The important details of providing and caring for the child are secure, for I have a good income and own a home.

Even though I have a supportive family and more than my share of wonderful friends, I cannot help but feel embarrassed and shamed by this turn of events. I need to be comfortable with the fielding of expected questions regarding marital status and the surrounding details, so that I may remain cheerful and hold my head high through the pregnancy. I feel no obligation to provide these details, but what can I say to colleagues and clients that is firm, yet not unfriendly?

GENTLE READER—Miss Manners presumes you are asking about questions that are well meant and within the bounds of what business people can properly say to one another, but she can't think of many.

"Are you married?" is not one of them. Perhaps "I suppose your husband is thrilled?" would be. But not what you gently call "surrounding details."

In any case, you should not be engaging in personal discussions on the job. This applies to married expectant mothers as well as unmarried. Not only is it unprofessional, but it encourages nosiness, the extent of which nowadays would astound you.

The proper reply for you to make to any such question is **"The child's father and I are separated."** Say it in a firm enough voice to indicate that the matter is not open for examination. And should anyone be so audacious as to ask why, the answer is **"Because we are living apart."**

THE MISSING WIFE

DEAR MISS MANNERS—My wife will soon be leaving our home to take a job in Washington, D.C. She will come home often (we hope).

What's a suitable reply to the inevitable "How's Susan?" "Where's Susan?" questions?

"She's left to work in Washington."

"She works in Washington."

"She lives in Washington."

"She's left to take a better job in Washington, and we're both nervously hoping the marriage survives."

None of these seems satisfactory. Suggestions, Ma'am?

GENTLE READER—Miss Manners feels obliged to point out that it is not customary to announce marital nervousness. It makes outsiders nervous. She also promises you that you really do not want to invite commentary about the wisdom of the arrangement and predictions about its success.

What your wife is doing is called commuting. What you should tell people is: **"Susan is fine, thank you; she is commuting to Washington."** How often she actually makes that commute does not change the situation.

As a native Washingtonian, Miss Manners can tell you that everyone in town refers to work as The Duty—or, for those of a dramatic turn, The Burden—of Public Service. Even those of us who just sit on the porch thinking of ways to make others behave themselves. And never mind that it might be a jolly good career move.

So if you are asked to explain the arrangement, you may add, **"Sure it's hard on us, but she felt—and I support her in this—that she really had to do her duty."**

ANSWERING FOR INFANTS

DEAR MISS MANNERS—What is the proper response to a question addressed at an infant? Several times, I have had people ask my four-month-old daughter, *"What a pretty baby—what is your name?"*

I have always responded, **"Tell the nice lady your name is Sally."** But how long can this go on when they then continue a conversation with the baby: "How old are you? What is your dolly's name? . . ." I am uncomfortable answering questions not addressed to me, yet feel I am being rude if I ignore the inquisitive stranger.

GENTLE READER—Although you got off to a charming start there, Miss Manners appreciates that there are only so many times an adult can manage to say "Tell the nice lady that . . ." When you begin to reach your limit, try dropping the ruse and answering the questions yourself. If that doesn't work, the polite phrase you need is **"Say 'bye-bye' to the nice lady."**

DAMPENING ENTHUSIASM

DEAR MISS MANNERS—My dear husband and I are in our seventies and active in our church. I am occasionally embarrassed when he becomes too active in extra civility.

He is an old rooster with young ideas. Whenever he sees an attractive hen in the church flock, he goes for her if she is receptive. Greetings between him and her are consummated by hugging, kissing and caressing, followed by mutually enraptured gazes.

I do not think they can make much whoopee because of

their ages. Nonetheless, their activism worries me. What can I do besides pray that they are not led "into temptation"?

GENTLE READER—You can join them. Not on the way into temptation, Miss Manners hastens to add, but by way of transforming his overtures into the appearance of sociability.

At the next opportunity, Miss Manners suggests that you slip your arm into that of your husband and, in a friendly and complimentary way, second his expression of admiration. There is nothing like a charming lady saying something like **"Tom, dear, do introduce me to your friend—my dear, I couldn't help noticing how pretty you are"** to kill a flirtation. Who knows, you may even make yourself a friend or two.

KEEPING A STRAIGHT FACE

DEAR MISS MANNERS—How does a gentlelady respond to a gentleman in a skirt? I encountered this awkward situation with my hairdresser, who says it is a new fashion. I am ashamed to admit that I reacted with cynical humor. We both ended up feeling offended.

GENTLE READER—Miss Manners is handicapped by not having been told the question to which the gentlelady was obliged to respond.

The answer to "How do I look?" is **"Wonderful,"** unless one happens to be the gentleman's tailor. In that case, a professional remark such as "They're wearing them a bit shorter this year, sir; shall I take it up for you?" might be in order.

INDEX